Killer Work from Home Websites

Blogging, Website Design

Website Business, Website Building

with

SBI Site Build It

Make Money Online!

Lee Evans

B

Brown Publishing

Killer Work from Home Websites

Published by Brown Publishing, New Carrollton, Maryland

Printed in the United States of America

DISCLAIMER. This publication is designed to provide general information regarding the subject matter covered. However, rules, regulations, laws, practices and the interpretation of same often change or vary from company to company, state to state, and country to country. Because each situation is different, the reader is advised to consult with his or her own advisor regarding that individual's specific situation.

Neither the author nor the publisher assume any responsibility for any errors or omissions, nor do they represent or warrant that the information, ideas, plans, actions, suggestions, and methods of operation contained herein are in all cases true, accurate, appropriate, or legal. It is the reader's responsibility to consult with his or her own advisor before putting any of the enclosed information, ideas, or practices into play. The author and the publisher specifically disclaim any liability resulting from the use or application of the information contained in this book, and the information is not intended to serve as legal advice related to individual situations.

This book is a work of the author's experience and opinion.

Learn more information at: Free-Job-Search-Websites.com

ISBN-13: 978-0615835730
ISBN-10: 0615835732

Table of Contents

Want More SBI!

Please visit my site here: http://www.free-job-search-websites.com/sbi-site-build-it.html. You can find out more SBI! info, ask me questions directly, watch the SBI! videos, or simply get started!

If you are as excited about SBI! as I was, contact me for a special offer before you sign-up with SBI!

http://free-job-search-websites.com/sbi-site-build-it-special-offer.html

Book Notification

If you would like to receive news about new book launches and free book offers, sign up here:

http://www.free-job-search-websites.com/amazon.html

Other Books by Lee Evans

— *Killer Work from Home Jobs: 200 Fortune 500 & Legitimate Work at Home Jobs*

— *Killer Work from Home Jobs 2: 100 Fortune 500 & Legitimate Work at Home Jobs*

— *Killer Work from Home Jobs: 460 Jobs SUPER* BOOK

Future Books by Lee Evans

— *Killer Work from Home Jobs for Bloggers*

— *Killer Work from Home Jobs for Writers*

— *Killer Work from Home Jobs for Information Technology*

— *Killer Work from Home Jobs International*

Dedication

To all those whose long passionate dream of working from home will be realized today.

Foreword

With the Internet going strong since half way through the Nineties, opportunities to make money online have come along for the ride as well. Just a plain web presence, the Internet has turned into a network of online businesses, in many different forms, using many different methods.

These days, small and large businesses cannot afford to ignore the Internet, as it has become a critical part of doing business. Where in the past, people would rely on the Yellow Pages to find local services, today, the Internet is for many, the first point of entry.

People do not just use the computer anymore to access the Internet. Take a look at any busy street in any city, and you will see people obsessed with their smartphone or tablet screens, while browsing the news, looking for information, leaving reviews for their favorite restaurant, or simply searching for information about a business.

Established businesses use Internet to expand their reach. Major brands sell in traditional stores and online, and the same is true for businesses that offer services instead of products. Other businesses do not have a traditional storefront presence, as those companies only exist online, benefiting from the millions of hungry customers globally.

You might have been in business for quite some time following a more traditional business model without having looked at online opportunities. Or... you might have looked into expanding your traditional business online, but you were overpowered by the wealth of information, preventing you from creating your first website or online store. It really does not have to be complicated at all, as Lee Evans explains, in this new book. But more about that, in a minute…

The time has come for traditional business owners to make the move to establishing an online presence for their business. Without it, your competitors will have the advantage, which is something you are certainly not looking forward to. Your business needs an online presence, and the solution for that is called SBI!

But maybe you are not a business owner, maybe you are caring for your child at home, and are interested in making some money to pay some of your bills? Not to worry! The Internet, these days, has opportunities for everyone to make money. The good part is that it does not require extensive knowledge, programming skills, or advanced graphic web design skills. It is far easier than that, and for a small amount of money, you can actually start as soon as today or tomorrow.

You might say, "But I am just an at-home mom, what do I have to offer?" The truth is that you have quite a lot to offer, and Lee Evans explains this through an example from a young girl who setup a tourist website that attracts more visitors than the average travel agency.

If you want to get an online sales stream going, and create financial stability, and a great future for you and your family, Lee Evans will show you which tool to use. This tool is inexpensive, easy to work with, and is used by many online businesses that are in the top 1% of visited websites. This tool has been proven to work over and over, and the best part is that you do not have to reinvent the wheel!

I am talking about a tool, or let us call it a system, called SBI! SBI! stands for Site Build It!, and is the most comprehensive tool available today, to create a professional website, blog, or online store with a few mouse clicks and a dream. Even a person who has limited knowledge of the Internet can use SBI! to create a stunning web presence. As Lee will show you through, numerous examples in this book, highly successful sites rely on the backbone that SBI! provides. Lee also reveals how she got in touch with SBI!, and what it took to create her first site (which is still in existence).

With SBI! explained by Lee Evans, there are no more excuses for you not to start adding or creating your online business. Do not worry, set your anxiety to the side, and mentally absorb what Lee has to tell you about SBI! Your website is almost complete, if you follow Lee's advice, while you get inspired by the stories outlined in this book.

Good luck with your next business endeavor, and I am looking forward to seeing your online presence!

Gerald Harris, MBA
Harris-USA

Introduction

Site Build It! (SBI!) is an unprecedented website and business building system. If you want to create a website that you use to show your latest pictures to your friends, SBI! might not be for you. Facebook might be the proper venue. If you are looking for an opportunity for a lifestyle change, one in which you create, and build a new vision for your future, then SBI! might be for you.

SBI! is an online software system, which helps you build a powerful website and blog; one that people love to visit, and search engines love to offer in response to visitors' queries. Once built, using a great site concept, search engine friendly keywords, information that you are passionate about, and content that visitors are hungry for, you can monetize your site, so that it will provide you with an income for the rest of your life.

This is a book about how I found SBI!, by researching the company, and falling in love with the product and the community. I noticed that there were a lot of people claiming that they had achieved life changing success with SBI! What I really liked was the fact that they were not making extravagant financial claims. They were simply saying that they made enough money to stop working at their prior jobs, and were able to turn their lives around. The lack of extravagance was what I found appealing.

These SBI!ers seemed like the person next door, regular folk; not the "Slick Willy" marketing guru, who wanted to sell his next million dollar coaching system, through a Thursday night webinar, guaranteed to make you a millionaire, too. The SBI!ers were moms, dads, retirees, employees, students and more, who wanted to redirect their trajectory, and create a future that was stimulating, exciting, renewable, and sustainable.

After some due diligence, I bought into it. I knew that if they could do it, it seemed reasonable that I could, as well. Somehow I had to suspend disbelief, until I made it happen. I had always been told that my work ethic was great, my performance was exceptional, and I always seemed to make things happen in my work life.

Well, this begged the question, if I could do it for these other companies (did I even know, or remember who the CEO was?), why couldn't I find something that I was passionate about and make things happen for me? Why couldn't I be the CEO of my own business? Why couldn't I make my life look the way that I had envisioned it?

Suspending disbelief is an important term. It was not always clear that I would be successful at achieving my goals. I went back and forth, at various times, about whether or not I would be successful. There were moments that I was full speed ahead, success is within reach, I can see that carrot, and I can grab it. There were other moments when I felt that I would never make it. During those moments, I relied on the strength and successes of others in the SBI! community. I suspended my disbelief, until my work reflected my expectations. There comes a day when you say to yourself, "They were right! It's really true. It's happening to me, too!"

My Story

I did not want to go to work anymore. It was as simple as that. I was tired of getting up early, driving or taking public transportation, spending hour after hour, at a job that just didn't matter anymore.

I felt that if I was smart enough to manage someone else's business, why wasn't I smart enough to manage my own? Enough was enough! I simply could not take it anymore. I decided that even if in the end, I was not as successful as before, any success would be worth being independent, and working from my home. It was time to do something new. The time was now, and there was going to be no turning back.

The first step in my journey, to work from home, was to find a job that would allow me to stay at home, and earn a reliable income. My decision was two-fold. I would find a work from home job, and while I was working from home, I would utilize that extra time, to create a business that would support me for the rest of my life. There was no turning back.

I invested every ounce of energy that I had, in finding a job that I could work from home. It did not matter how much I made, as long as it paid my bills, and gave me the time I needed to start my own business. I have not looked back, since I made that decision. D-day, also known as decision-day, was the first day of the rest of my life, a decision that I am still excited about, as I sit at my computer right now.

My Transition

First, I found a home-based job, and worked for a company as a telephone customer service operator. The money was significantly less than I had been used to, but I came to the realization that how much you make is not as important, as whether your life looks the way that you had always imagined it. My life was taking shape, but I had only just begun.

The next step in my journey was to create a business, which would finance my life and fund my dreams. I explored many options. It was important that I not fall victim to a scam, or other illegitimate opportunity. The

Internet is a wonderful place, filled with golden opportunities. But it is also a place of many dangers, and I did not want to be yet another headline.

I proceeded cautiously in my travels, and exploration of various possible directions. I actually stuck my toe into a lot of ponds, on my way to my final destination; but as I traveled, I found the idea that kept rearing its beautiful head was SBI! Site Build It! No matter where my explorations took me, I found that I would bump into this name, again and again. What I also noticed was that there was a lot of "good press" about it. Not really press from the newspapers, but, it just seemed that people who tried SBI! were everyday people like me, who were all genuinely excited about the lives that they had created for themselves.

The feeling I got from my research was these were real people, who had simple dreams they turned into businesses, which served as the foundation for their new lifestyles. I felt as though I was joining a club, or a community of people, who shared the same hopes and dreams, for a future that they actually created themselves. The people were not millionaires it seemed, (although nothing is wrong with that). They were just everyday folks, able to convert their former lives into new lives of self-reliance. These new lives now revolved around family. Why? These SBI!ers now had more time to spend with their loved ones. In some instances, they started new businesses incorporating their loved ones, so they got to share their success, and make it a family affair. Let's check out a few more success stories.

SBI! Success Stories

Elad Shippony

As I considered the possibilities of using SBI! to fuel my dreams, I was introduced to Elad Shippony's story. Elad, who lives in Isreal, is an infopreneur, which simply means he makes money on his website, by selling information to others. Elad, and his sister Tamar, have created several kids birthday party sites. Their main site, www.coolest-kid-birthday-parties.com, is number 164,207 on Alexa. They are in the top ½ percent of all the websites in the whole world. They were not technically savvy, they simply created their business using SBI!

The highly profitable business provided, both Elad and Tamar, a major source of income in under six months. Elad has monetized his business, by placing Google's AdSense ads, affiliate products, and creating finder's fee arrangements, based purely on the content that the pair placed on their sites. This means the brother and sister pair do not have a product, and they do not deal with customers. Elad and Tamar do not service clients. They simply create high quality content, information people seek, and their business now supports their lifestyle.

I was very impressed with Elad's story, but I continued to look for more case studies, then I found …

Crystal Maleski

Crystal's story, like Elad's, was appealing because of its simplicity. She's a mom of four teenagers who loves to cook, and she bumped into her work from home business by accident. Crystal said that she reads cookbooks, like everyone else reads novels. (In my non-cooking world, this concept is unimaginable). Her friends would contact her about dinner ideas. The list of requests became so long, she figured other people might be interested in her ideas too.

This is how her SBI! site http://www.makedinnereasy.com/ came about. Crystal has over 1,600 people visiting her site daily. In addition, she has

7,500 subscribers to her weekly newsletter. Businesses are now contacting her to be a social media consultant regarding how to effectively use Facebook and Twitter.

I really loved Crystal's story, but I wanted to forge ahead to see what other SBI!ers were doing. My appetite was whet, so I dug a little deeper, pounded the pavement a little harder, and then I found …

Shaun Fawcett

Shaun's story, once again, was appealing because it's about a man that had a dream, who turned his long-term dream into a reality late in life. Shaun was a government administrator, who longed to be an entrepreneur. He reminded me of myself in a way, a person trapped in a career they shouldn't be doing. As Shaun said, "… for all of those years I was actually the spirit of a small time entrepreneur, trapped inside the mind and body of a government administrator. In many ways it was a difficult, soul destroying, and spirit extinguishing experience. Arghhh!" I totally get it Shaun! Your mind, your soul, and your spirit are dying, a little bit at a time.

One day he saw an article in the paper that referenced Dr. Ken Evoy, the founder of SBI! The article stated that Dr. Evoy was considered a worldwide expert in helping everyday people, to create a work at home business online.

Shaun decided that this was the opportunity he had been waiting for, so he purchased SBI! and used it to figure out what the best choice was, for following his passion, and determining the best option for a successful business. He used Brainstorm It!, an SBI! tool, to analyze the likelihood of success of a few of his business ideas. Shaun chose practical writing help as the niche for his website, because he enjoyed writing, and he was good at it. He created http://www.WritingHelp-Central.com. Now Shaun has 10 ebooks that he sells on Clickbank, and he offers writing courses, to over 160,000 people around the world in over 160 different countries. Above all, his days as a government administrator are over!

Nori Evoy

The most prolific SBI! success story is Nori Evoy. Nori is the daughter of Dr. Ken Evoy, creator of Site Build It! Her website, anguilla-beaches.com, is a travel site that focuses on the beautiful island of Anguilla. Nori started her site when she was 14 years old, and the site has evolved over time, to have a higher traffic ranking than some of the islands major hotels, or the official Anguilla Tourist Board site.

Like all of us, Nori used Brainstorm It!, one of the many tools SBI! offers, to identify the best, most profitable keywords. Her website is a perfect example of what you can achieve with SBI!, by simply selecting a profitable niche, and providing quality written content that continues to draw people back to the site again and again.

Nori has monetized her travel site in a number of ways, with the help of an arrangement her father developed, she gets paid for real estate leads from a local realtor, who has sold houses, rented lots of villas, and even sold land on the island, through visitors from Nori's site. In the case of the land, it sold for $3,000,000, and Nori received 10% of the realtor's commission. She also gets paid for boat charters, cars rentals, and Google Adsense advertising fees. Nori earns thousands of dollars per month operating her part-time travel business. She has had the site over 6 years, and is now 21 years old.

These are just a few of the people that have influenced me to choose SBI! What I loved about them was that they were just regular people, starting regular websites, which turned into regular businesses. These businesses allowed them to follow their bliss, work from home, and change their lives. I will supply information at the end of the book that will provide you with an endless supply of everyday people success stories, if you'd like to know more.

What is SBI! Site Build It!?

Dr. Ken Evoy

SBI! Site Build It! is a software tool that helps everyday people create websites with quality content, which they can convert into online e-businesses. Dr. Ken Evoy, the founder of SiteSell Inc., is the creator of this all-in-one system, which enables amateurs and pros alike "… to build online businesses at unprecedented rates and levels of success."

Dr. Evoy has created a number of successful products that have sold internationally, including numerous software products. He created this breakthrough website creation tool, because he believed that everyone can be empowered to craft quality theme-based sites, which can become income producing businesses. He is respected by Internet authorities worldwide for the Sitesell brand, and his belief in ensuring a quality-driven product, which is both affordable and "OVERdelivers" to his customers.

The Company

Sitesell Inc. is headquartered in Montreal, Canada, and was founded in 1997. The company has over 40,000 SBI! customers, and over 80,000 affiliates. The website is an Alexa Top 500 site, which means that it is one of the most visited websites in the world. For good reason, SBI! has members in the United States, Canada, South America, Europe, the Middle East, Asia, Australia and Africa. When you become a member of the SBI! forums, you might find yourself talking to your next door neighbor, or someone from the global community.

I needed to hire someone to help me with a design item, after some research, I found him in the SBI! forums. Once I started dealing with him, I discovered that he was living in New Zealand. I loved it!

SBI! is the company's flagship product. It is a business-building system, which provides users with keyword brainstorming research tools, viral traffic building components, and incorporates over 85 site creation, hosting, and marketing functions, in its proprietary site building technology.

What are SBI!'s Features?

SBI! is a website builder that focuses on giving you the processes and tools needed to convert your site into a profitable online business. But what exactly are those processes? What are the tools? Well, there are so many tools and processes available to you, it will take a while to quantify everything, but here goes!

The Action Guide

Probably the most important tool of all is the Action Guide. The Action Guide is the step-by-step guide that tells you everything there is to know about SBI! and how to do it. It is comprehensive, intense in its detail, and it is considered THE most valuable tool in the SBI! arsenal of technologies by most of the SBI! community. The Action Guide is the soup to nuts compilation of how you will accomplish creating your successful business. The guide exists in a variety of formats, including written, video and mobile.

Support

SBI! provides a phenomenal support group that usually responds to your questions within hours. They are there to help, and they do. I have probably asked every question that can be asked, and with the help of Jill, Carol, Erika, Cheryl and more, I have gotten answers over the years to the questions that mattered most to me. Those responses have always been given respectfully and with a smile (an email smile).

Commitment to Updates

SBI! is constantly being updated. They recently performed a $3 million overhaul of the BlockBuilder (BB2) software system, so that it has the latest and greatest capabilities. BB2 is SBI!'s second generation webpage builder; a simple block-by-block approach that makes building a website, which search engines love, a simple task.

SBI! also keeps you updated on all the issues that you need to be aware of, so that you do not need to waste your time digging around, or trying to comprehend every new concept that comes along. The latest news and issues in the world of technology, that impact our sites, is thoroughly researched by SBI! and provided in the most appropriate format.

As they say, "Everything is **all** in SBI!. ***All*** the tools, ***all*** in one place. And ***all*** for one low price." To be quite frank, they provide so much information, I simply bow out of the information mill and focus solely on my business. If it starts to get "loud," then I look into it, because it is simply more information than I need.

BAM

BAM is what YOU bring to the table. BAM is short for Brain, Attitude and Motivation. Brain means that everyone knows something. Do you know about Chihuahuas? Do you know about travel? Do you know about car repair? Have you had health issues? If so, then you know about it. There is someone out there that wants information about what you know.

Attitude means that you have a "can do" spirit. Somewhere down deep, you know that you have what it takes to achieve your goal. My feeling was, if I was a business success for others, why couldn't I be a business success for myself? It was my fundamental philosophy that wound up being accurate.

Motivation means that you have the determination to persist until you succeed.

If you want to build a successful business that will sustain you year after year, you will have to bring BAM – brain, attitude and motivation to the table. This is true whether you are creating a business online or otherwise.

The SBI Process

The PROCESS

SBI! provides you with the preparation you need, a proven process **C -> T -> P -> M** and all the tools you need, and this combination equals business success. SBI! has a proven track record of successful home businesses created as a direct result of the combination of preparation, cutting-edge tools and state-of-the-art processes. But what exactly is this process?

PROCESS: C -> T -> P -> M

Content – people use the Internet to find information. Whether they are researching prices, heath information, how to make money, or looking for the latest fashions, people use the Internet to find the answers to their questions. If you provide them with the answers to their questions, you will be rewarded by Google and other search engines with traffic. Providing high quality "content" is the key to your business success. When you provide high quality "content" people see you as an information authority (so do the search engines). As the quantity of your quality "content" increases, your traffic increases.

Traffic – once the search engines (ex., Google, Yahoo! MSN), realize that you are consistently providing high quality "content" they begin to reward you with high quality "traffic." This free targeted traffic is the lifeblood of any website. Your traffic, otherwise known as visitors, also known as future customers can be delivered to your website in the thousands per day. The more targeted visitors you have, the more future customers you will have. SBI! has the largest amount of sites in the top 3% of the worlds sites created by regular everyday people. When your site has thousands of unique visitors per day, some of this "traffic" becomes PREsold. You provide them with what they are looking for, the information is premium quality, and they become PREsold.

PREsell – this process occurs when strangers that visit your site, read what you have posted and develop trust and confidence in you. Why do they develop trust and confidence? The visitors read pages and pages of the high quality "content" that you are OVERdelivering and you become an authority. Provide them with the answers to the questions that they have, like prices, heath information, how to make money, or the latest fashion information, and a psychological bond is created.

How do you deliver high quality "content"? Simply provide information in your own voice, in your own style, in your own way and your visitors will start to trust you and then like you.

Monetize – now that your PREsold visitors trust you, many will convert into ready-to-buy customers. You monetize your site by converting your warm, willing-to-buy visitors into income. Search engines will deliver you free targeted traffic, month after month, year after year. All you have to do is blend I multiple streams of revenue, and your business will continue to grow and will support your lifestyle year after year.

The C -> T -> P Motor

The C -> T -> P process is the motor of the SBI! engine. If you follow the step-by-step process faithfully, your engine will drive the P to the M. Your PREsold visitors will be driven to monetize your site, year after year. But what are the SBI! tools that help drive the engine?

SBI! Tools

The TOOLS

The SBI! tools are broken down into implements that help with preparation, site building and hosting, traffic-building, trust-building, monetization, guidance and support. Let's explore each …

TOOLS: Preparation

In order to create a sticky website, one that draws and retains traffic, you have to identify the keywords that your visitors search for in your niche, you need to know your competitors and how to deal with them, and you need to plan how you are going to monetize your site so that you can earn the most money possible through your website.

Brainstorm It! Version 3.0 is the SBI! tool that you will use to identify the topics that will pull your website visitors to your site. You will be able to see exactly which topics are the most profitable and which topics are of little or no value.

Brainstorm It! will help you to identify your Site Concept based on your areas of interest. If you love sail boats, you will discover the best angle to approach a business based on that concept. It might be profitable to teach people how to sail a boat, it might be more profitable to offer information about the best locations to sail a boat around the world, it might be more profitable to offer information about the businesses that cater to sail boat repair. There are as many angles as you can imagine when it comes to selecting your Site Concept, and Brainstorm It! will help you every step of the way.

Brainstorm It! provides an advanced option that allows you to intensify your research beyond the basics. When it is said that Ken "OVERdelivers" trust me, you will understand the meaning of this if you decide to become a part of the SBI! community.

SiteSell Supply is a ground-breaking tool that tells you about true competition. When you know about your competitors, you are able to make informed decisions about the best content to create so that your site winds up in the top 3% of sites, like many other SBI! sites.

Site Info provides you with the competitive information that you need for any keyword or domain. The information is summarized from over 2,500 sites on the web. It is a priceless piece of competitive research.

Alexa Integration is built into SBI! providing you with an unending supply of invaluable competitor information.

Search It! is a tool that provides you with answers to questions that you have about your competition, about monetization, about vital statistics, about legal research, about images and much more. The tool has over 100 advanced searches in over 20 categories.

Niche Choose It! is the tool that helps you to choose the very best Site Concept possible for your site. Are you going to create a site about how to sail, or how to diet, Niche Choose It! will help you to identify the very best choice that also fuels your passions.

TOOLS: Build & Host Your Website

Here is where process and tools consolidate. The **C -> T -> P -> M ->** process is an integral part of the SBI! mix of cutting-edge tools. What does this mean? Simply, the process drives the need for certain tools. In the case of building and website hosting tools, content is in the driver's seat.

C stands for content. You may have heard, in the online world of traffic seeking, that 'Content is King." Content IS King, and it represents the aspect of website building that you will need to focus on most, to be a successful business owner.

SBI! provides you with all of the things that you need so that you can focus on the most important part of web building, which is content building.

Domain Name Registration is a part of the process. SBI! will register your domain name for you, and put it in your name. Click a button and you are done. There are no additional charges.

Web Site Hosting is part of the process, as well. I have never heard of an SBI! site going down or being inaccessible. In addition, you do not have to pay for hosting. Hosting is included in SBI! Unlimited pages, images and bandwidth.

Name Park It! is a means of saving a domain name that you might be interested in, but do not intend to use at this time, or for some other reason. If you want to protect a certain domain name, then simply Name Park It!

Creative Site Design Tools allow you to design your site without having any design skills, simply select a pre-built site design, in your choice of 2- or 3-column layout. You simply add your logo text and you are on your way. You will be able to customize your site using the Site Designer, which you access through your browser. You will be able to create your one-of-a-kind site by using the personalization features, including colors, fonts, textures and effects.

There's an endless supply of customizable templates which have been created by a variety of website designers so that you have an endless supply of looks for your site.

If you are a skilled designer, then you can create your site the way that you want it to be. You can use CSS, Photoshop or you can upload your own HTML.

Block-by-Block Page-Building that's simple, but powerful, will make site page creation a cinch. BlockBuilder 2 (BB2) is a simple and painless way to create beautiful pages that your visitors will love and the search engines will love, as well. You can drag and drop the parts of the page that you need. Will you include an image on your website page? Just drag and drop the image block. Do you need to write a few paragraphs about your sail boat, just drag and drop the text block. Do you need to create a link to another page? Just click on the link builder and you're done.

BB2 is built for those with limited or no website building experience. If you've never built a website before, once you learn the simplicity of BB2, you will begin creating websites that look like they were professionally prepared. You may have an introductory learning curve, as is true with anything new, but you will begin to build pages like a true Pro.

Are you an advanced Webmaster? Then, simply …

Use Your Own HTML Tools if you are skilled and want to create a design yourself with Dreamweaver, Photoshop or CSS, then all you have to do is upload your pages into SBI! and your site will look exactly the way you designed it. So, in addition to having your custom site, you will be able take advantage of all the other incredible tools that SBI! offers to help you build the best business possible.

Page and Image Managers will help you control your pages and images by simply using your browser. No need for FTP

Content 2.0 is really quite incredible, if you use Content 2.0 with the pages that you create, your visitors can create web pages for you, so for each one page that you create, you can invite your visitors to make comments, add pictures, give their opinions, tell stories, or do whatever you think of. Why is this important? If your visitors build pages, your site will grow exponentially (without any additional effort on your part). The more pages -> the more traffic. The more traffic -> the more money!

Here is **Mantius Cazaubon's** story about using Content 2.0:

"I have seven SBI! sites and have added Content 2.0 on 6 of them. I have a total of 3,102 C2 pages on my sites.

I see C2 as a way to put one's site on auto-pilot, so to speak. My sites keep updating all the time.

My sites get found for so many terms. Some C2 pages outrank pages that I built myself!!

With real people posting and interacting on a website, it makes the site look so much more genuine to first-time and even long-time visitors. One of my

C2 sections, about lyric feedback, is so loved by visitors, it's almost unbelievable.

C2 helps to differentiate my site from non-SBI! sites. They simply don't have this feature. It's a must-have.

C2 is the best form of leverage I've come across online. Visitors submitting content for free? What more can you ask for?"

Mantius Cazaubon

electric-guitars-guide.com

Automated Blogging you can turn your web pages into a blog without any additional work. SBI! will automatically convert your website pages into blog format and will create an RSS feed. Your visitors can simply subscribe to it. Just click a button and you're done.

Regular Blogging is also available, if you want to attach a WordPress or Typepad blog to your site, you can. But it is not necessary. If you want to, it is available to you.

TOOLS: Traffic Building

We learned that the **C** in **C -> T -> P -> M** stands for content, and that SBI! provides you with an abundance of tools to make your "content" exceptional, for human readers (so that more and more readers will come and stay) and for search engines, so that engines like Google will recognize that you have great content and will, therefore, send you more traffic.

The next step in the business building **C -> T -> P -> M** process is building targeted traffic. This is the **T** in the **C -> T -> P -> M** process. Traffic is the lifeblood of any website. If you do not have traffic, then you do not have visitors, if you do not have visitors, then you will not make money. It is as simple as that. Any successful online business has a consistent flow of targeted traffic that arrives at their site daily.

Some businesses pay for traffic, through AdWords or through paying high "rental fees" at major portals. SBI! helps you to develop a "sticky" site that causes visitors to effectively "stick" to your site, by coming back again and again. In addition, SBI! helps you to create a site that causes Google to determine that you are "sticky," as well. The more that Google likes you, the more free targeted traffic you will receive.

SBI!'s processes and tools are specifically created to help you to develop a website that brings you loads of targeted traffic, so that you can monetize your site and earn a great living. The **T** in the **C -> T -> P -> M** process is what every website owner wants - Traffic. SBI! delivers by providing a cornucopia of tools with the sole purpose of ensuring that if you write quality content, quality targeted traffic will be delivered to your site. What tools?

Analyze It! is a tool that analyzes your web pages prior to posting them. This amazing tool lets you know if you have created a great page. It tests whether your page addresses everything needed to meet the requirements of the search engines, so that you can get free traffic.

Automatic Sitemap Creation submits your site to the major search engines so that it can be indexed promptly, and, so that the engines can go about the business of delivering traffic. SBI! ensures that this is taken care of, so that you can focus on what's most important, your business.

Automatic Search Engine Pinging ensures that each time you update your web pages with changes, all major search engines are notified, so that they have the most current information. Your sitemap includes your images, so search engines are pinged when you change your images, too.

Automatic Search Engine Tracking advises you when the search engine spiders have visited each of your pages and when each of your pages are listed in the search engines. SBI! even reports if the engine is taking too long to list you, or if your page is dropped by the engine, and provides you with suggestions on how to take care of it, should this situation occur.

Search Engine Ranking Reports tell you how your pages are ranking for your specific keywords. If the pages are not ranking well, the report makes recommendations on exactly what to do.

Traffic Stats are presented on a daily basis. Each day you will know how many unique visitors you had the previous day, and which web pages are bringing the most visitors. In addition, you get information on which keywords are bringing visitors to your site. If you prefer to use Google Analytics, SBI! sites are compatible.

SBI!'s Click Analysis provides information about visitors who click into and out of your site. This valuable information is critical to understanding user behavior and how to heighten your monetization process. The better your monetization, the more money you will make.

Pay-Per-Click Acceleration makes each pay-per-click campaign you decide to initiate a cinch, instead of the troublesome brain-numbing experience it can be.

Value Exchange promotes link exchange between complementary third-party sites. This gesture is one that is appreciated by the search engines. Your visitors benefit, you benefit and your partners benefit. A number of SBI!ers have said that Value Exchange has also lead to additional opportunities, like joint ventures.

Private Traffic Headquarters state-of-the-web resources, such as Search Engine HQ, Value Exchange HQ, Image Search HQ, Local Search HQ, as well as Video Search and Shopping Search provide the most up-to-date information that you need. These features provide the functionality to generate additional traffic and to keep you abreast of exactly how you are doing.

TOOLS: Trust Building

The next step in the **C -> T -> P -> M** process, or the **P** is called PREsell. You build trust in the people who visit your site by providing them with the quality information that they were searching for. When you OVERdeliver, by giving them the answers to their questions and more, you create a relationship. Your visitors begin to see you and your site as a good, reliable source for honest information. The relationship deepens as the trust relationship expands; as the relationship grows, your visitor becomes PREsold, a warm and willing-to-buy customer. You then become a "Brand of One." When people trust you, they will buy from you. The more you PREsell your visitors, the more you enhance the trust relationship, the more customers or buyers you will have.

What are the tools that strengthen that trust relationship?

Blog It! turns your website into a blog. So there is no need for a blog site, although, if you want one, or have one already, that is not a problem. It simply means that you don't need one, because Blog It! turns your website into a blog for you automatically, so that you can focus on what's important – your business.

Socialize It! is a marketing tool that allows your visitors to share their excitement over the great information that they are getting from your site with their friends and family. Socialize It! is a set of social media buttons for Facebook, Twitter and others, that you can place on every page you create. When people share information with those they love and care about, it can go viral, thus increasing your traffic.

In addition, Socialize It! has HTML code that webmasters and bloggers can post to their sites if they want to share information that you are providing. This helps you because it increases the backlinks to your site. The more backlinks you have, the more of an authority you are perceived to be by the search engines. The more of an authority you are, the more traffic you will receive.

Face It! allows your visitors to "Like" your website pages or "Like" your website as a whole. Face It! also provides a commenting tool which allows anyone to add comments to your pages, and allows Facebook users to post the comment to their wall for all their friends to see. Another marketing tool, the more that people share the quality information that you are providing, the more visitors you will have.

Face It! offers spam control, so that you do not have to worry about people entering damaging information, just set the level of control you want and then forget it.

Face It! helps you to tap into the almost 1 billion user market of Facebook, to expand your visitor reach, by allowing your visitor's friends and family to trust in you, because their friend or family member essentially provided them with a testimonial about your site.

Facebook's Open Graph Tags are another benefit used by Facebook, Google, ShareThis and other social media companies (I don't know a lot about it, other than to say) open graph meta tags allow you to control what content shows up when your page is shared on Facebook, or other sites.

Pin It! is a tool that allows your visitors to pin your photos to their Pinterest boards. If your site is image laden, then this would be a great tool to spread the word and gain some link juice at the same time.

Twitter Follow Button – if you have a Twitter account, your visitors can follow you on Twitter with just the click of a button.

Google +1 Button – if you are a Google+1 believer, and you should be, you can get your pages to rise to the top of the search results with Google+, also, Google+ users are able to start a conversation about your page.

Pinterest Follow Button – lets your visitors follow you on Pinterest. It's as easy as one click.

Newsletter Publishing helps you to continue your relationship with your visitors. You can deliver more quality content through the creation of an e-zine. It's another trust builder. Remember, when you develop trust, your visitors will buy from you, and will come back, again and again.

When you create your e-zine you'll get **SpamCheck!** You don't have to worry about your e-zine being perceived as spam by Yahoo!, Hotmail and other ISPs. You will get full information on what to do to make sure that your e-zine gets through.

In addition to **SpamCheck!**, you get **OpenRate** which lets you know how many of your subscribers opened your e-zine and the percentage. It is a window into the minds of your subcribers.

Form Build It! / Autoresponder is a data collection and auto delivery system. Form Build It! allows you to gather names and emails, feedback, survey information, polls, leads and more. You can earn referral fees for leads that come into your site from visitors, and have those leads sent to a partner.

The autoresponder can auto reply to information gathered, or you can create a course by way of a series of scheduled emails. All part of the PREsell process that enhances your credibility and enhances the relationship between you and your visitor. Every point of contact strengthens the trust building process.

Link Fix It! ensures that all of the links on your site are functioning properly. If the Link Fix It! bot finds a link that goes astray, you will be advised, so that you can update, or remove the link. Why is this important? Having a quality site is not just a matter of the content that you write or the colors and images that you choose. Part of building trust and credibility is having links that go where they are supposed to go. It is part of the customer experience process. In addition to building trust, search engines like sites that do not have broken links. Broken links mean customer or visitor frustration. No one likes that.

Mail Services such as email, webmail, Gmail, and more, are at the ready. If you prefer to use online or desktop email software, you can. If you want to use SBI! WebMail, it's available to you. If you prefer the Gmail interface, you can send and receive SBI! mail through Gmail, using your SBI! domain name as the return email address. You have many options available.

TOOLS: Monetization

The monetization step is the money step. It is the **M** in the **C -> T -> P -> M**. Everybody loves the monetization step because it is the reason that we are all here. We want to build a business that will be successful, a business that will not only support us now, but will support us well into the future.

If you want to look at it this way, all the SBI! modules are monetization modules. Brainstorm It! shows you where the most profitable keywords are. Search It! can find almost anything that exists on the web, if you are looking for affiliate programs that offer products in your niche, Search It! is like calling the cavalry. Form Build It! will allow you to broker leads to partners for a commission. All of the SBI! modules are geared toward one thing, creating a profitable business that will carry you well into your future.

Private Monetization Headquarters is the place where SBI! owners find out how they can convert the traffic that they have generated into a fist full of dollars. When many of the SBI! sites are in the top 3% of traffic sites, we need to know how to "*maximize per-visitor income* by establishing and growing *multiple streams of income.*"

Monetize It! is a three part module. It is divided into content-building, ad-selling and PPC-buyng. Content-Building finds high profit opportunities that are in sync with your web site's theme. Ad-Selling helps you to earn the highest payouts for your ad income. PPC-Buying is a little different, it shows you how to buy PPC in the most effective way, however, most SBI!ers don't buy PPC.

Infin It! allows you to plug in third-party resources into your site's subdomains. There are an endless amount of possibilities from ecommerce stores, to course training modules, to community forums, to blogs, to wikis or membership sites. If you can think it, you can incorporate it into your business.

The SBI! forums is an incredible place to explore the possibilities. Other SBI!ers share information about what they have added to their sites. Taking time to read the amazing things others have done is part of the fun. Your world will open up far beyond your initial plan of just having your basic information site. Everything that you need, to become a successful work from home business, is at your disposal.

TOOLS: Guidance & Support

All of the modules, videos, technology and more, that SBI! provides is still not all. You are not alone. There are many helping hands available to you to help you along the way. There are thousands of people who have come before you and we really are a community. Some are more active than others. Some lurk, some are leaders, but either through your questions or their maverick answers, there is someone who is exactly where you are in the process. There is a village of caring hands to help you along the way.

I am not one of the biggest participants in the forums, but when I need to know something, there is often someone who has posed the question before me, with an answer waiting for me to read. If I can't get what I want from the forums, there is an always vigilant group of support helpers to answer my quirkier questions.

The Action Guide is like taking a course, it is a step-by-step guide to everything that you need to do in order to accomplish your business building goals. The process is clearly and cleanly expressed, so that if you are an amateur, or a pro, you will understand it. You can choose to read it on your computer, mobile device, or watch a video. I chose to watch the video, however, some have actually printed out the Action Guide, and highlighted it with yellow marker. The choice is yours.

Integrated Online Help is available as you go through the process of building your website. As you build your page, you can find out the answers to questions that you might have as you go. The answers will appear in-context.

SBI! Xpress E-zine is delivered regularly, about four times a month. It contains interesting items that you may want to know about, and other things that you need to know about. You do not have to keep up with technology, because everything that you need to know is right there. The information is usually discussed in two ways, the brief way, and the detailed way for those who want more. Are you too busy to read it? Not a problem. There information is there for you if you want it.

Tips 'n Techniques Central contains great articles that always give me a new perspective on things. Sometimes they are from the forums, SBI!ers who have achieved the most success, sometimes they are from Ken Evoy, but the articles are always enlightening information with pearls of great wisdom geared toward helping you make the next incredible step.

Resources Headquarters offers the best-of-breed third party tools that can save you time and money. There are a lot of tools available, and you know that they have been rigorously reviewed by the SBI! staff to ensure quality.

SBI! Private Forums are a blessing. Next to the Action Guide, it is the next best "tool" in the SBI! arsenal of tools. Thousands of people who have achieved success are there to offer you a hand, a suggestion, a new idea, a pat on the back, or another point of view. The forums, filled with the SBI! community, is priceless. SBI! refers to the forums as "*The* Place For Friendly, Success-Focused Discussion." It's also a place that some people just hang out, to be around like-minded members. If you want to know about it, it is probably there.

Unlimited Customer Support is available to you twenty four/ seven. I don't think that I have asked a question they have been unable to answer.

TOOLS: Recent Additions

SBI! is constantly upgrading, and adding new, cutting-edge features to the technology. It seems that I am always receiving a report that there is a new, fabulous feature added to the product. Honestly, it never ends and you couldn't possibly use all the features, but they are there if you need them. The very definition of OVERdelivery, at its finest. Here are some recent additions to the SBI! feature lineup:

Pinterest Follow is now available, just add the button to each of your web pages. All you need to do is click, make a few adjustments, and your visitors will be able to follow you on Pinterest.

Pin It! is also available for images on your site, it will allow pinners to pin your images.

Open Graph Tags are now added to all SBI! web pages. Facebook, Google and other social media companies use this to aid in site social visibility.

Google +1 buttons are now available for web pages. This button allows your visitors to vote for your page in Google and Google+. It's as easy as a click and a few adjustments.

Twitter Follow buttons are now available for your web pages. Just add your Twitter handle.

BlockBuilder 2 (BB2) is the new drag and drop browser-based page builder. It's intuitive and easy to use.

Site Designer controls the look of your site, there are 200 templates to help you select the look that you like.

AdSense It! Content 2.0 is a monetization module which allows you to add Google AdSense to your Content 2.0 pages, allowing you to make money on the pages that your visitors create. There are an infinite number of placements for the Google ads, which helps to maximize your income based on the size of the Content 2.0 page.

Brainstorm It! V3.3 the newest version of Brainstorm It! has been released.

Content 2.0 Multi-Image now allows your visitors to add 4 photos to their Content 2.0 contributions. The more that your visitors can customize their pages, the more they will share the creations they are proud of with their friends, more friends = more traffic for your site.

Priority Build It! allows you to tell the search engines which pages on your site are the most important with a click of a button.

Sitemap XML File - SBI! works your sitemap, and along with auto-pinging, ensures that your web pages get into the search engines fast, and makes sure they stay there. All spider visits are tracked, and SBI! even checks to make sure that your pages are indexed in the search engines. Search engine rankings for each page are reported, also.

Image Search Report – if you have a site that is image based, then this 2 level report will give you all the information you need to increase your image based keyword results, this can bring you even more traffic from Google. It's like icing on the cake.

What Types of Businesses?

Google AdSense

Google AdSense is the easiest way to monetize your site. If you do not want to deal with customers, do not want to deal with hard goods, do not want to create digital products, and don't want to offer services, then placing Google AdSense ads in strategic locations on your website can be a very profitable and incredibly easy way to make money.

This type of monetization model is called passive income. Why? Because all you have to do is create great content and Google, and other search engines will reward you with traffic. Once you have traffic, Google will reward you even further through AdSense, by posting ads on your site that some of your visitors will click on. Some website owners make thousands of dollars per month as a result of Google AdSense, with no other monetization model on their site. But why stop with only one monetization model?

Affiliate Marketing

Affiliate marketing is another great form of passive income, like Google AdSense. There is no need to create products, you do not have to buy and store inventory, you do not need to handle customers, you do not need to process credit cards, you do not need to ship products and you do not have to handle returns.

If you decide to select this marketing model you simply select a product that is complementary to your site's concept, post the product and wait for your affiliate commissions to add up, month after month. There are many companies that act as stewards for affiliate programs, like ClickBank, Commission Junction, LinkShare, Google Affiliate Network and ShareASale. When you join an affiliate network like Commission Junction, you know that you will get paid for your referrals, because they get paid also. So, Commission Junction, and other well known networks, make sure that the infrastructure works perfectly. The only thing that you would need to do is continue to create high quality content, so that your site grows bigger and bigger, increasing its authority on the Internet, thereby increasing your income, year after year.

Allan Gardyne, owner of AssociatePrograms.com conducted an experiment to see how a couple of site would do, with little investment of time or effort. Here is his story.

Allan Gardyne

"Hi Ken …

… A Part-time Project that Keeps on Earning

Speaking about longevity, it's time for a quick update on the two SBI! sites Rupert built back in 2002. After all these years and facing new competitors by the boatloads, they're still earning a nice little income every month.

The 2 sites have settled into an income level of about $2,000 per month, solely from affiliate commissions and AdSense.

That's despite this being a passive project where an assistant, who is thousands of miles away, provides part-time maintenance. There's no sign of a recession in those figures!

I reckon it proves what a fantastic job you do with the instruction manual, videos and SBI! forums.

SBI! Remains My Top Recommendation

After all these years, I still tell affiliates to get SBI!, not just because of its package of smart tools, but also because of the incredibly comprehensive education SBI! gives you in how to build a business online.

It's good to see that you're getting SBI! into more and more colleges and universities. That clearly illustrates how special SBI! is.

Even a Few Hours of Work Produces Results

Ken, I was thinking about how I started my SBI! sites as experiments. My main business keeps me way too busy, so these days all we do is add an occasional new page to the sites.

It's a great example of what someone can do with just a few hours a month (if that). If we had the time to really invest and push these sites with all your tools, we could multiply these results.

It's all About Perspective!

I realize that my latest income figures may not be as sensational as some of the others on the case studies site, but I feel they're good examples of what someone can earn with a very limited, low-hour effort. I sure don't mind earning an extra $2,000 per month!

You've played a huge part in our freedom to travel and enjoy ourselves while other people are busy working. Thank you!

Life is good, Ken."

Allan Gardyne
AssociatePrograms.com

Auction Sellers

If you are an eBayer, and eBay is your only stream of income, then you will find that you are supporting eBay. You create the listing, you pay for the listing, you respond to the customers, you pack the products, you ship the products and you have to accept returns. In addition, you have to live with their rules.

But, what if you had a website with multiple streams of revenue? This does not mean that you have to stop placing auctions on eBay, it just means that you can create a number of income streams, in addition to eBay through diversification. Create a passive stream of income that supplements your eBay activities. As your new SBI! empire grows, you will find that you probably have more customers on your website than you do purchasing from you on eBay. I know, because I used to eBay, and it is no walk in the park! Here is Amy's story.

Amy Dykens

"I had long wanted to run my own business and had some practical experience in managing a gift shop, but my husband's career as a college football coach means we move often.

These moves are usually positive moves for promotions and better situations for him, but that reality made the dream of becoming an entrepreneur seem unattainable for me for many years.

In 2004, I started researching opportunities to open a business online. Internet businesses were growing and expanding and many people, including me, were becoming more comfortable ordering items online.

Enter eBay...

With such low start-up costs, low risk, and millions of potential buyers in the form of built-in virtual foot traffic, I was sold. I could finally open my gift shop and become the entrepreneur I had always wanted to be and still be mobile. When we moved, my business could move with me.

I worked hard and grew my business for the next year. I carefully expanded my product lines and revenues to become a moderate success with my eBay auctions and my eBay store.

One morning, I logged in to see if anyone had purchased from my shop while I was sleeping (which happened often) only to find that I was out of business. All my hard work, careful planning, and growing revenues were wiped out in the night.

Someone, probably a competitor, used the "report this listing" feature to tell eBay I was selling a recalled and, therefore, a dangerous item. The automated computer response system, in place to protect consumers, shut down my store and closed all of my auctions. I was suspended from eBay until the problem could be resolved and *my store was closed until further notice from the powers in charge at eBay.*

I was losing money every minute that I was shut-down and I had been shut-down on a false accusation with no questions asked. The item reported was not a recalled item at all, but the eBay computer system didn't know that and the extended eBay organization is too gigantic to investigate each item reported before acting to protect the consumers from such items.

Of course, this is how eBay must handle these situations to protect themselves and their shareholders from any legal liability. The eBay community is usually very supportive and honest and this type of thing doesn't happen very often, we hope, but it did happen to me.

I cannot express the frustration I felt and how sad I was to realize eBay had so much control of my business. After two weeks of emailing and faxing, because talking to a real person was impossible, I was cleared and my account reinstated. I was free to go on about my business; eBay was willing to let me continue working for them.

To say the least, this experience was frustrating and scary, but also an eye-opener for me. Running a store on eBay goes beyond leasing space at a "virtual mall"... I pay to be on eBay for some very good reasons like traffic, advertising, and reputation, but they are also taking their cut of every sale and they are completely free to tell me to get lost at the drop of a hat.

This wasn't what I had in mind when I envisioned owning a business. *I was supposed to be my own boss.* The experience taught me unequivocally that I was relying too heavily on someone else for the success of my business and absolutely had to diversify. I wasn't building something that could stand on its own; I was building equity for someone else, eBay and its shareholders.

After much research and comparison, I chose SBI! to help me share my passion for beautiful beaches. I also saw how it could help me expand my business and begin to build my own traffic.

When I started with SBI!, I had no idea that it would take me from being fairly happy selling small gifts, to fulfilling the dream of traveling to exotic beach locations!

I have not abandoned the eBay model. It is lucrative and useful, so I keep it, for now. I utilize my eBay store to embed my products into www.beach-therapy.com, but now I'm using eBay to send traffic to me while also generating traffic of my own.

If I decide now that the fees I pay to eBay are no longer worth the traffic and convenience of their offerings, I can simply cease to use them. eBay no longer has the power to summarily close my business; I would continue to grow and function without them.

Having my own website also increases my credibility on eBay and helps me convert the traffic I get there into more sales. It is a very effective strategy to capture as much of the market share as I possibly can. eBay sends me traffic and when I send them traffic they pay me as an affiliate for doing it. To say the least, my business has grown and prospered since I stopped working for eBay and started using SBI! to grow something that is truly mine.

My "About Me" page on eBay directs traffic to www.beach-therapy.com and every customer who buys from me receives an automated email message inviting them to visit my SBI! site and to sign up for my newsletter. I am able to convert these visitors from eBay customers to my own customers.

eBay now works for me, rather than me working for them. And my SBI! website converts more of the expensive traffic I buy from eBay into customers than my eBay "About Me" page ever did on its own.

In addition to hard goods, I have expanded into other income streams, such as affiliate links and Google ads. eBay restricts these other strategies very tightly and I lost money on clicks in the past. Now my *About Me* page sends me traffic from eBay that I can monetize in other ways, even without a purchase.

The resources I received with my SBI! site, the Action Guide and forums, taught me how to generate my own traffic, something eBay never wanted me to do.

In 2006, I was able to expand and hire a part-time employee to help with packing and shipping and with emails and questions. She also happens to be my sister and it is fun and rewarding to work with her. We leased a building to move operations out of my house and continue to grow each year.

I have to say that the business trips have also improved immensely!

Before SBI!... working in my basement, packing and shipping.

After SBI!... working on the beach in Florida, Aruba, and Mexico!

I'm living my passion and SBI! gave me the tools to do it. Thank you, SBI!."

Amy Dykens
beach-therapy.com

E-Goods

E-goods are electronic products, like ebooks, software, database products, art, cartoons and illustrations, e-music and sounds, and digital mobile phone products. Kindle is the best example of a digital product distributor, other great examples would be iTunes by Apple and Google Play. If you decide to become a digital product seller, once you have created your e-goods, you have no product to deal with, there are no products to pack, and you do not need to ship anything.

Your SBI! website can be your distributor or you can choose a distributor, like Amazon or ClickBank, to process your orders, deal with customers, process credit cards and returns. I am an example of an e-goods business owner. You can find my contact information at the end.

Existing Online Businesses

How is your existing online business doing? SBI! has some tremendous statistics to support the success of member websites. Remember, these statistics are about everyday people, like you and me. These are not website gurus, information technology engineers or webmasters extraordinaire. 35% of SBI! sites are in the top 1 percentile, 53% are in the top 2 percentile and 62% are in the top 3 percentile of all websites worldwide. There are over 100 million websites globally. When you look at the full picture, these are stunning statistics.

You will not jump into the top 3% the day after you start. You will have to build your site. Some sites arrive at that number faster than others. It depends on your subject matter, keywords and skill level. But if you stick to "the processs," utilize "the tools" and stick to the plan religiously, you too can become a statistic. Targeted traffic is what all website owners want, because targeted traffic, turns into motivated, interested, willing-to-buy your product visitors. SBI! delivers the holy grail for websites, which is traffic.

When you compare Nori Evoy's website anguilla-beaches.com, which has an Alexa ranking of 43,753, with anguilla-vacation.com (the Anguilla Tourist Board's official website), which has an Alexa ranking of 9 million, you begin to realize the power of SBI! Alexa ranks sites from number 1 to in the millions. So the lower your Alexa number is, the more traffic your site has. So let me restate this, a teenager built a website that has more traffic than the Official Anguilla Tourist Board. Enough said!

Hard Goods - E-commerce

Do you make or manufacture your own products? If so, then you are a hard goods seller. You may be selling online now, but, are you selling to your capacity? No. If you do not have an SBI! site, then you are not. As a person that sells hard goods, you are called an e-tailer, and your online store is called an e-store. If you are currently operating an e-commerce site, then you need SBI! so that you can move your site into the top 3% of traffic rankings in the world. Targeted traffic equals buyers. Maximize your traffic and minimize your cost of acquiring customers.

In the offline world, the way that you get customers is through location, location, location. Online, the way that you get customers is through information, information, information. If you provide high quality information, your visitors will find you, become interested in what you have to say, and become PREsold, ready to purchase buyers. The Internet allows the world to be at your doorstep. Why sell your products locally, when you can sell to the world?

Louann Shenberger

Here is Louann's story in her own words. "I began working in a flower shop in late 1994. Although I did all kinds of design work, my heart was in love with wedding flowers. I eventually found myself managing a full time shop, plus handling all the wedding work.

Health began to catch up with me as I was diagnosed with fibromyalgia. I couldn't take the long hours and heavy lifting, so reluctantly I resigned my position in the fall of 2006.

I was eager to begin caring for my first grandchild, but knew I should be contributing to our finances as retirement loomed over my husband and me.

Where Could I Earn Money?

I doubtfully approached the Internet - my experience being limited to some casual browsing on it. I toyed with the idea of selling through eBay, but a short experience with it convinced me that eBay was making a lot more than I was!

When I stumbled across SBI!, I was extremely skeptical at that time due to all of the "get rich" schemes being touted on the internet. If it was so easy to make thousands on the internet, why were they bothering to show them to me?

SBI!, on the other hand, seemed different. In fact, their sales page seemed to caution that if I was looking for fast money, this wasn't for me! Their "sales pitch" made a lot of sense to me, cautioning that it took time and skill to build a quality business. (I was cautious enough to visit the BBB first, making sure there were no complaints against SBI!.)

I liked the fact that I could actually e-mail real websites directly and ask their owners what they thought of their SBI! experience. These people seemed to have nothing to gain personally by responding to me and this seemed a lot more real than those "quotes" you see on the other sites! Laura from Cheap-Chic-Weddings.com responded to my e-mail immediately, with a friendly manner and warm enthusiasm for SBI!.

Convinced that SBI! was for real, I wavered on clicking the "Buy" and committing myself. $299 seemed like an enormous investment for me. But I took a deep breath and plunged in, already knowing that I wanted my niche to be built around wedding flowers. That was my area of expertise and passion.

Every Journey Begins With One Step

While I threw my hands up at first, declaring I would never understand how to build a website, I persevered. Despite some pretty big "oops" in the beginning, understanding of the process began to sink in. My Home Page was finally published on May 2, 2007.

Unlike many others in SBI!, who plan their "M" in monetization around Google Ads and affiliate programs, I knew my niche would have to include providing specific hard goods to my visitors. Since I focus much of my attention on teaching my visitors how to create their own wedding flowers, I also knew that many of the supplies were not that easily available or accessible to them.

Having my own online store was the best solution for my brides and me. Because I was so busy, I had someone set up my store's framework, while I worked on my information site. I knew that it was going to be the main traffic generator for my store.

I began with over 400 basic products used by florists for weddings. My first step was to compile a list of the products I actually wished to carry in my store. I then had to meet with my wholesalers to determine wholesale prices, which then had to be marked up for retail.

Whew! It is a daunting task and I can see why SBI! suggests it's easier to have an information site with Google Ads for income. Yet it's been immensely satisfying to build a business one step at a time. I learned the ins and outs of a small warehouse (set up in a basement) and how to pack and ship like an expert.

Sales and More Sales

My first year in sales were over $12,000 and **the following year I more than doubled it with over $32,000 in sales.** I anticipate continued growth and have had great satisfaction in knowing that my business is growing by leaps and bounds.

The best part? I showed enough progress to convince the manufacturer of my hottest selling products to refer me to a florist wholesaler who is now helping me to take my business to the next level. Because he drop ships my orders, this means that I have access to a warehouse full of products that I don't have to spend a dime on until I sell them! It is pretty much unheard of in the floral industry for a wholesaler to be willing to break cases and do the shipping for you, while giving you the rock bottom case price on all your products.

How did I do this? It was because my traffic on my SBI! site was impressive enough to convince a major manufacturer to want to work with me, personally initiating contact with a wholesaler several states away. I've since flown twice to meet with my wholesaler, hammering out details and meeting with the people who are joining me in my vision for a successful online business.

Dreaming Big

SBI! allowed me to step out of my comfort zone, putting my skills to work in front of a computer rather than in hauling and lifting all those water buckets for flowers. Since my site went live in May, 2007, I can now definitely say that *my income has more than doubled since I was working full time... and I am anticipating huge growth in the coming years.*

My unique visitor traffic keeps expanding (one day my unique visitor stats actually broke the **10,000 benchmark**) and my potential for growth looks better each time I build a new web page. **My pages have been viewed well over eight million times in the last 12 months.** That adds up to a lot of Google Ad "clicks" and climbing passive income (with about a 4% Click Through Rate or CTR).

God has blessed me greatly by leading me to SBI. I will never say the learning curve was easy (many times I felt like pitching the computer into the swimming pool!). But I've met so many wonderful SBI'ers - many thru e-mails and several by phone. I actually met one who is now a dear friend. She even offered her hospitality to me when I flew to her state to meet with the wholesaler.

I still have so much more to learn but I have a great many plans for my baby company!

My advice to everyone I meet? Demand a lot from yourself. Dream big, set high goals and don't let anyone deter you from them."

Blessings,

Louann Shenberger
wedding-flowers-and-reception-ideas.com

Infopreneurs

Elad Shippony

Here is Elad's story in his own words. His words represent his status when he started out. He has been an SBI!er for years now, and his success has continued to eclipse his original levels.

"Following up on last month's awesome results, I'd like to share with you this month's phenomenal stats:

-Last month www.coolest-kid-birthday-parties was ranked 117,705 (Alexa). Today, one month later, the site is ranked 59,340 and moving up by the day.

-Over $4,700 in sales (and over $600 in commission)

-More than 14,000 visits (more than 10,000 unique) and over 38,000 page views

-More than 8,000 click-throughs to affiliate sites

-Almost 250 newsletter subscribers

-I can go on and on.

I'm already starting to build the concept for two new SBI! sites and plan to get them running next month."

Elad Shippony
Elad from Coolest Parties
Israel
coolest-kid-birthday-parties.com

Elad's Update

And the next month's happy report …

"My fourth month into SBI! generated almost $6,000 in sales and broke the $1,000 mark for COMMISSION! The site is ranked 50,821 and I've got close to 500 subscribers to my Birthdayography newsletter.

Oh yeah, and during August I was also on vacation for a whole computer-less week of Scuba diving in the Red Sea while my site continued to work as usual.

Without a doubt, SiteBuildIt! is It!

P.S. You've just heard what I have to say about YOUR product. You should hear how MY visitors love MY site!"

Elad Shippony
Elad from Coolest Parties
California, U.S.A.
coolest-kid-birthday-parties.com

The above statements were made when Elad had one website, coolest-kid-birthday-parties.com, Elad now has 8 sites, all under the "coolest" brand. That's cool! (sorry!)

Local - Offline Businesses

How can a local small business with only a few employees, that's a "brick and mortar" business benefit? Local businesses need new customers to succeed. If your business is located near Grand Central Station, you are probably not reading this book. Otherwise, local businesses need a way to secure new customers without having to pay for customer acquisition, through advertising.

SBI! can be the new, cost-effective way to secure new customers. Who can benefit? Real estate agents, lawyers, landscapers, gas stations, restaurants, bagpipers, manufacturers and grocery stores, to name a few. Any local business can benefit from more customers.

Kristen Mcclure

Kristen Mcclure is a newer, local SBIer. Here is her story, in her own words:

"I started my SBI! site because I work about 55 hours a week on my therapy practice.

I love my job but I'm exhausted and frustrated because of the volume of clients I have to see in my office. Managed care has essentially destroyed psychotherapy. We have to work so hard for so little money.

My plan is to create some other sources of income and attract higher paying clients through my website. The point is to see less clients, for more money, so I don't go crazy.

I have only just begun building my site but am so excited! To make a long story short, yesterday I received three referrals from people in my area who had found me through my website. These three clients were higher paying clients, the kind of clients I want to attract.

My clients love my website! I can point them to different pages that are relevant for their situation. The kids in my practice enjoy making artwork and creating poetry that I put on it. I love writing new information to help the clients and parents I work with.

The three new clients will pay for SBI! in one week! This has been such a great thing for me, I never anticipated it would be so helpful and satisfying. In the long run I think SBI! will save my job and enable me to keep helping people into retirement."

Thanks to SBI!.

Kristen Mcclure
kristen-mcclure-therapist.com

Judd Burdon

Judd Burdon is another local SBI!er. He has been around for a while. Here is his story.

"I own and operate a small asphalt business. My business was focused locally until I started to use SBI! to promote my business.

As you can understand, treating and sealing driveways and making repairs to asphalt is really something that has to be done physically and therefore the local focus.

However, when I started working on my SBI! site, I realized that I could take my business to a new level and reach out on a much broader basis. My knowledge and understanding of my business allowed me to create very interesting content that would be relevant to consumers and do it yourselfers as well as small contractors. It didn't take me long to realize that I could develop my own affiliate referral program where folks that were looking for a reference on someone in their area would come to me for that reference.

Also, I saw the opportunity to apply all my learning around the kinds of equipment and supplies that it takes to run a small asphalt business by offering the equipment for sale on my site. So I packaged up my knowledge with some excellent equipment and now I market it as a "business in a box" solution where someone interested in starting up their own asphalt treatment business could come to me for a turnkey step by step solution, from the equipment and supplies through to the business plan and spread sheet pro formas.

There is no question that SBI! has changed the way I look at my business and my future. I now understand how I can take my knowledge and package it up and reach a worldwide audience. A great example of this is the recent inquiry that I received from the Contracting Officer of the Contracting Squadron of the U.S. Armed Forces in Bishkek, Kyrgyzstan…

"We are looking for commercial items to take care of the runway here in Bishkek, Kyrgyzstan. An asphalt router/saw and a hot pour crackfill applicator. As you might imagine it is in poor shape so these machines will be getting a lot of use. Thanks in advance for your assistance."

Yes, the U.S. Army! All the way from a third world country that I've never heard of. What amazing reach! (My site beats many much bigger companies at the engines, scoring in the top 150,000 at Alexa.)

Thanks for something that allows me to take my local business, repackage it, and sell it to the world. It has added an entirely new angle and revenue base."

Judd Burdon
asphaltkingdom.com

Judd has changed his business from a local concern, to a worldwide enterprise. Why? SBI! allows each of us to expand our horizons in ways that we may not have considered otherwise. SBI! provides the process, the tools and the community support to help you expand your business beyond your wildest dreams.

Network Marketers

Are you in network marketing? Are you in someone else's downline, while you are trying to build your own downline? Companies like Silpada, Pampered Chef, Amway and Shaklee, represent the new breed and the old guard of network marketing companies. In network marketing the holy grail is targeted leads of people who are interested in buying your product, joining your downline, or both.

SBI! can help you generate sales and find warm, pre-qualified leads, acting as your lead generating machine 24 hours a day, 7 days a week. There is an additional benefit with SBI! because once you have acquired your targeted PREsold downline, you can then teach your downline how they can do exactly what you did. Teaching your distributors to replicate your success will be doubly profitable. How? By becoming an SBI! affiliate yourself, you will receive commissions on your downline's marketing efforts with SBI!, as well as your earnings with your network marketing company. This will become a double dip in the commission earnings game. You can build a earnings machine that will turn into passive income in no time.

Does your network marketing company provide you with a website? Possibly. Your site will look exactly like everyone else's site. Same look, same words, same ineffectiveness, but they do not provide you with leads. They will want you to buy leads or figure out a way to get them on your own. That network marketing website will sit there doing nothing year after year. Ask your network company if they provide you with leads. Ask them right now - I assure you they do not!

What if your network marketing company wants you to buy a website that they will make for you. It will surely be an expensive proposition. Once again, your site will look like everyone else's site, same words, same content, but what you probably don't realize is that it will not have any visitors. You will still have to generate the leads on your own. How will you be able to get visitors to your site?

SBI! is specifically made to teach you how to generate targeted leads, or visitors who will be PREsold and ready to buy your products, take part in your business opportunity, and rinse and repeat your exact efforts, based on your success.

Passion

Passion simply means that there is a site concept that you want to create because you love the subject-matter so much, you have no choice. For example, if you are a day trader and it is your passion, and you find that you must have a site on day trading, your future has already been determined. The financial arena is a particularly tough nut to crack. There are likely several lucrative approaches to the financial industry, but you insist upon the one that is in the most competitive field. Well, you know what you are going to do. It will not be easy, and you may, or may not reach the traffic levels that others have achieved, but you are crazy happy!

Welcome to my world. Helping people to find jobs is my passion. In my opinion, there is nothing else that I could do with as much passion and conviction. However, when I started my website, Free-Job-Search-Websites.com, I discovered that the way that I wanted to approach the topic meant that I would be in a highly competitive field. This meant that I could eventually conquer the site concept subject matter, but it would be a fight; and it was also possible that it would take so long, that I might never conquer it.

My passion drove my decision. I felt that as long as I was doing what I love, everything would be alright. The road to success has been a slow one, and it will likely continue to be slow, but I am working from home and most importantly, I am crazy happy!

Real Estate

If you are a realtor, then lead generation is the lifeblood of your business. You need new people who want to buy, and new people who want to sell. It is very likely that your company's website is not providing you with the leads that will allow you to excel at the level that you dream of. The Internet is a vast harbor of potential buyers and sellers.

I do not know a single real estate buyer or seller who does not get on the Internet in order to research the property or properties they are interested in. It is at this moment, the moment that your potential buyer is looking for information, that you can become the information provider. Once you provide your potential buyer with the information they seek, the trust relationship begins to build. It is in this moment that your visitor transitions from traffic to a PREsold buyer. You have given them what they want for free. The information that you have provided answered their questions.

The visitor realizes that you have provided high quality content. The targeted visitor begins to see you as an authority in your field. The relationship grows and the inquiries roll in. Name recognition and client trust are the variables that a lead generation machine will build for you. The Internet provides a goldmine of opportunities to the real estate agent.

SiteSell Inc is an Approved Education Provider by the Registrar REBBA 2002 (Real Estate and Business Brokers Act 2002) and SiteSell Education's course *"Building a Successful Real Estate Business Using the Internet"* is approved as a Training Program by the Registrar, REBBA 2002.

Which agents can benefit most?

Well established agents interested in increasing business growth or entering a new business niche.

Agents relocating to a new town or market who want to jumpstart their career in a new city.

Newer agents who have a small or no client base at all.

Listing agents for a new construction community who are responsible for selling numerous properties promptly.

Agents who want to quickly grow the listings side of their business to show potential sellers.

How can agents use SBI!?

Buyer attraction systems: Attract more buyers. The vast majority of today's buyers begin their real estate searches online. These buyers will frequently preview online listings and review valuable information for months before they ever begin their search for an agent. Why not be the Web site that helps them reach all these goals, while also positioning yourself as the clear agent of choice?

1. Lead capture systems

2. Drip marketing systems

3. PREselling systems
4. Lead qualification systems
5. Listing marketing systems
6. Seller attraction systems
7. Niche marketing systems

If you do not have time to invest in the process of starting your site, SBI! can do the work for you. SiteSell Services (more about this below) will eliminate the initial learning curve, and get your site off to a great start. All you will have to do is continue creating your high quality content.

Referrers & Finders

A referrer or a finder is a middle-man, or woman. The referrer finds for others what "the others" do not have, or need more of. A referrer is an intermediary, and fulfills a basic and time-tested function in business. Who is a referrer? An example of a referrer is a scout that has an eye for discovering "the next" modeling talent, the most successful and recognized faces in the industry.

Another example of a referrer is a person who finds buyers needing loans for mortgage companies. The finder will receive a finder's fee from the mortgage company and can make a great living if they can continue to provide what the mortgage company needs. The possibilities are endless.

How can you earn your fees? Here are a few ways:

- pay-per-sale *commission* — each sale that you make will earn you a commission
- pay-per-sale *profit* – in a resale setting you earn a profit
- pay-per-lead – each inquiry will provide you with a fee

- pay-per-click – like Google AdSense, each click will earn an income stream

- pay-per-month – your company receives a monthly fee

Retirees

Retirement is something that most of us look forward to. We make plans to have a great income in our golden years. Sometimes the best of plans don't work out the way that we intended. Sometimes those plans work out, but we want something to wake up to every day; something that will inspire us.

SBI! is a way to help you retire with an additional income stream. You can create a new income that will either supplement or exceed your fixed income, or other earning streams. In addition, you'll have a new and exciting business that you can be proud of. Is there anything better than a business you have developed yourself, that pays your bills, gives you something to get excited about, and gives you the wherewithal to do the things that you have always wanted to do? Hardly!

Sue Spires

"SBI! means friendship, community, family, caring, and learning how to do it right to make money. SBI! also means the pleasure of building a quality website that is #1 on Google and Yahoo and getting over 1000 unique visitors a day. I'll keep at it as long as I can remember how to run on my computer. Hey, don't forget I'm in my 70's!"

Sue Spires from
freepatternsforstainedglass.com

Travel

Here is an SBI!er with a big passion for travel, this is her story:

B. Bradtke

"My biggest passion is travel. Freedom, adventure, and new experiences. My biggest fear used to be that life would pass me by while I'm busy paying the bills.

I used to frequently day dream about becoming a travel writer. In reality, I was stuck with a less than inspiring day job, a sizable mortgage, and the fact that English is my second language.

When I started reading about SBI!, suddenly something, which for years had seemed like such a lofty dream, was right in front of me. Here was a chance to write about travel and earn money with it, and I didn't have to be a Hemingway to do it. I didn't know anything about websites, but I knew a life-changing opportunity when I saw one, so I jumped at it.

Now I have two SBI! sites. Both are growing and making money. The most important aspect for me is not the money though. It's the freedom SBI! gives me.

Freedom

It's always been my goal to be able to spend at least 6 months of the year traveling. With SBI!, I can do that. I can pack the laptop and go for 12 months! And should I want to move again, I can do that too, without worrying about finding employment.

Thank you for making it possible! You saved me from my biggest fear. Life is not passing me by."

A grateful nomad,

B. Bradtke
outback-australia-travel-secrets.com

Here is the story of Fiona McCardle and Jim Andrew, another SBI! family success story:

Fiona McCardle & Jim Andrew

How did "Rent a Villa in Tuscany" (our Web site) end up in the top 1% of the Internet and how did two Scottish designers end up living in a medieval village on top of a hill in Tuscany?

It's all Sophia Loren's fault! Well, sort of! If her childhood next door neighbor, Paolo, hadn't moved to Tuscany and if winemaker, Paolo, and his family hadn't renovated a farmhouse on a hillside and if they hadn't asked us how they could find rental clients for the farmhouse, then we would never have started "Rent a Villa in Tuscany".

In a strange way, all our previous experiences, which at first glance seems a million miles away from what we are doing now, were actually good preparation.

Both Fiona and I are art school graduates in Textile Design. For many years we ran our own knitwear design studio in a warehouse on the banks of the River Thames in London. It was probably around this time that the seeds of our fascination with Italy were sown. Over the years, we've also built up experience in sales, customer service, technical support and photography. These skills, combined with our fluency in Italian (we've now lived in Italy for 14 years), led us to look into the possibility of setting up a web based villa rental business.

Like thousands of other people round the globe, we'd read all about the power of the web and how it was possible to run a totally flexible, international business from a computer in your front room. Great, but the big question was, how?

OK, we were creative and I had played around with some programs designing a web site with photos of Rosie, our baby, but I didn't have a clue how to start setting up a "proper" site.

It was at this point, late one night, surfing through the thousands of "get rich quick" schemes on the net that I came across something that stood out as being very different, written by a Canadian Doctor called Ken Evoy. The product was called “Site Build It”.

Maybe it was something about his friendly style of writing, maybe it was because it seemed to include everything (and more) I was looking for but right away, I whipped out the old credit card and instantly hesitated! It seemed “too good to be true”. More research was needed.

I checked out their independent results page (very impressive). I checked out the opposition. Again, SBI! left them all standing. I even checked out respected “web gurus”, Ralph Wilson and Jim Daniels, who both gave SBI! top marks. I had nothing to lose (SBI! has a money back guarantee) and everything to gain. Little did I know at that point that we were about to set out on one of the most exciting, bizarre years of our lives.

So what’s happened in the last 12 months?

a. We’ve been invited round to world famous designer Salvatore Ferragamo’s villa (you can now rent it from us for your summer hols!)

b. Whilst lounging by a swimming pool, a Hollywood production company called on the mobile wanting “the biggest villa you have for 2 months” (we thought it was a friend winding us up)

c. We’ve been asked to organize a mega wedding bash for Chuck Berry’s ex-piano player’s son. Only one problem! Can the Guinness tanker get up the hill?

d. A world famous New York photographer asked us to find a venue for his Tuscan photo course.

e. An award winning journalist from a quality, Irish tabloid, the “Banbridge Leader”, wants to do a feature on us. We reckon he just fancies a free holiday!

f. We get daily calls from beekeepers, gardeners, carpenters, fashion designers, chemists, pizza makers, cheese makers, winemakers, web designers, piano players, 2nd hand car salesmen, and others who just happen to have a 14th century castle or two lying around, all desperate to be on the site.

g. Last month, folks from over 60 countries looked at almost 30,000 pages of our site and we're not even finished building it yet.

Sounds like a dream! But the most bizarre thing of all is none of this would have been possible without SBI!. Sure, we were hungry, motivated, hard working, determined, had design skills, people skills and liked working with computers. We had researched our market and knew it had potential. BUT we don't have an exclusive on any of these. So why did we do it when 98% of small business on the net FAIL. What makes SBI! different?

In one word, TRAFFIC.

Most (almost all) small business web sites (some are even very pretty with all the latest bells and whistles) sit out there in cyberspace all alone, no one ever looks at them.

A web site that no one looks at is a very expensive hobby!

The owners wonder why!

There's nothing magic about SBI!'s servers, of course. It's all in the step-by-step logical process, and the tools that "do" the process. SBI! doesn't just give you the tools to build a web site, SBI! helps you build a successful web business. As I said, I checked out the Net completely, and I had never seen a page of success stories like SBI!... and now we are on it, too — one of the top-ranked sites (sorry for bragging a little).

The process is just so logical... Content - Traffic - PREsell - MONETIZE.

Starting with content (after all, that's what people search for, so that's where we begin, too). Right from the start, SBI! showed us how to brainstorm our idea to find out if it was valid. It helped us choose and register our site name. Then it supplied the tools to create a content rich themed site, which the search engines love.

Since the traffic-building is built right into the content (thanks to more SBI! tools), you have the TRAFFIC. "But I'm not a techie," I hear you say. SBI! is child's play.

If you can put one building block on top of another, you can build a top ranking site. The materials are written using a user friendly, step by step method. When your site is up and running, SBI! also has a newsletter mailing program (you have signed up, haven't you?), saving you time and allowing you to get on with writing great content.

And how do we know we're doing it right? We use "SBI! Site Central", which analyses, submits and tracks our pages, giving us all the essential information we need to tweak our site to top position on the net.

Once you have the traffic, your site gives your visitors what they want. Answers. Solutions. Information. And that is what PREselling is all about.

Now that you have warm, happy visitors, you are ready to MONETIZE that traffic. How you monetize will vary according to your business. We do it by renting villas in Tuscany!

Yes, it's a tough job, but someone has to do it.

It's so logical, so efficient, and the tools make it so do-able. But you still have to do it. While SBI! made this possible, we built this business. So if you are looking for a get-rich-quick, Dr. Evoy would be the first to tell you to chase after these false dreams elsewhere. If you want to own a business that makes it fun to wake up each morning, I can't say enough how much SBI! has impacted our lives.

I love to talk about SBI! and I love to rent villas in Tuscany! So if you'd like to do either, you can reach me at…

rent-a-villa-in-tuscany.com/contactus.html

I always felt safe because SBI! has a no quibble, money back guarantee. They even let you keep the domain name if you don't want to continue. Who would ask for their money back on a product like SBI!? Those seeking the holy grail of "get-rich-quick" — remember, you are really building a genuine business of your own here. As long as that is what you want to do, you'll love it — but they refund you, no questions asked.

Do your homework, research the market (we did). You'll find nothing that compares to SBI!.

What does the future hold for us? We've almost finished building "Rent a Villa in Tuscany," we're about to take on help and we're already working on ideas for another site. Meanwhile, I'm busy fending off email from people pleading with me to tell them "how we did it".

Every now and then whilst sitting in the shade of an olive grove sipping on a glass of Chianti, one of us will say "can you remember how this actually started?" so much has happened in the last 12 months. Yes, it's taken some work, but SBI! turned the "impossible" into "done."

Without a doubt it's been one of the most satisfying years of our lives. Instead of getting all nostalgic about the past we are more excited about plans for the future, adding new luxury properties, working on a new "Tuscan Thermal Springs" page and one of our most exciting projects is investing in new wi-fi mobile technology.

If you'd told me 12 months ago that a couple of ex knitwear designers with very little experience of the web would now be running a successful web based villa rental company I'd have found it hard to believe. If you then tried to convince me that their plans are now to run it from a poolside, looking out over the Tuscan hillside, sipping on a cocktail, I'd probably think the Tuscan sun had got to you!

You know what, up until a year ago, before I found SBI!, I would have been right. But we jumped in "with both feet," as Ken says...

And now ......cheers!

Fiona McCardle and Jim Andrew
Italy
rent-a-villa-in-tuscany.com

Sales & Rentals

Jerry Mack

Here's the story of Jerry Mack in his own words:

"Ken,

You may not realize it (although I suspect you do), but SBI! is much more than "the only all-in-one site-building, site-hosting, and site-marketing product" (I think that's what your site says!). It's actually a "9-to-5 life liberator."

Of course, I wish I really knew that before I tried it, as my story will tell.

In my former (pre-SBI!) life, I was a regional manager for a medical imaging company. My headquarter's website was just not getting us any new customers (or leads). And that's how my first SBI! website started.

Starting from scratch

I needed a way to generate leads to help me sell medical equipment in the office I had just opened in California for a medical distribution company based on the east coast. Basically, I figured that if I had control over web-based sales promotions and marketing programs, I could build sales significantly in my region. Otherwise, I was going to starve, because their expensive, fancy, gorgeous site was not sending me any business at all.

I built my SBI! site with some pages based on keywords from the brainstorm tool in SBI! and also built pages where the keyword was the model number of the products I sell (so obvious, yet so powerful). The pages I built based on keywords from SBI's brainstorm tool brought in traffic from my general target market. The traffic came because these keywords were in high demand by web searchers and not supplied by many websites on the net. The pages I built based on product model numbers brought in traffic because they were usually ranked very high in the search engines — and that traffic, while lower, was super-targeted.

SBI! submitted these web pages for me and then managed them to the top of the search engines rankings. You know what's great about being as "Net-dumb" as a guy like me? I just trusted SBI! to do its job, while I did mine! (I'll bet you get some smart tech-types who try to outguess SBI! — HA! HA!)

And boy, did SBI! ever do its job. Anyone entering specific keywords, for example their specific model ultrasound machine (talk about a highly targeted lead!), finds my site at the end of their search. It really works well.

I was often ranked higher than the website of the company that manufactures the products I represent. In my business, this creates a lot of hot leads that usually turn into sales. And with a new customer ordering supplies, that means a significant future revenue stream as well.

SBI! really is the ultimate sales person's tool

Ken, I know you like to show Alexa rankings as proof of how well SBI! works, but people want to know how that translates into dollars. Yes, I know your sites explain how small businesses have to build the traffic first through great content, PREsell it and THEN monetize it, but people still want to know "how much money that Alexa ranking makes," if you know what I mean!

And that goes triple for us sales guys! So let me cut to the chase. My Alexa traffic ranking made it into the top 80,000, well within the Top 1% of all sites on the Net. What did that translate into, in business and dollars?

SBI! worked so well that I built a brand new sales office (with zero sales) to one with over $250,000/month in less than a year. In all, before I left them, I sold millions of dollars worth of product, at a 10% commission.

Actually, it worked a little too well (as far as head office must think, anyway). Why?

Well, I recently resigned from that medical distribution company because it was obvious I didn't need them. The company was getting the benefit of all the sales generated from my SBI! traffic.

And here's the funny part. Head office couldn't understand how the heck my little site was generating all that business. The HQ Webmasters thought I was just lucky. (And I'll bet that's what they told management — after all, they had to be doing something mysterious and difficult to earn their salaries, right?)

As Rodney Dangerfield would say, "I got no respect." Meanwhile, I was wishing I had known that SBI! would work this well before I took the job and started the site. And then it occurred to me — "You know it now, so what are you going to do about it, Jerry." (I don't usually talk to myself, only in "EUREKA" moments.)

EUREKA! The Epiphany

I wanted to try it for myself, own my own business and my own life, so I went for it alone. (Well, not exactly alone, I also had my wife and SBI! — but never ask me to choose between them.) I knew that I could generate all the leads I need to make a living on my own.

And yes indeed — my new company is already doing just fine because of the SBI! website, which is barely underway but already pulling leads - www.sonomahealth.com. Sonomahealth.com will grow to be the cornerstone of how I earn a living as an independent medical distributor selling ultrasound systems and supplies at my new company, Sonoma Health Products.

Actually, I'm more of a broker or a sales agent than a distributor. To my customers, though, I look like a large national distributor with multiple warehouses across the country.

In fact, I do use several warehouses across the country, I just don't have to tie up any of my money in owning inventory because I let the "old school" distributors do that. I am a virtual distributor, a modern-day sales agency - as you can see, the actual inventory that I maintain fits into my garage!

I do my business successfully because I use Site Built It!. And I'll be the first to admit I don't even use all the features and capabilities of SBI! to their full extent. SBI! is such a powerful tool you just have to "kind of" know how to use it to be successful.

So because I "kind of" know how to use SBI!, it helps me make me a very nice living in a company of my own. (Yes, I am one of those famously "lazy sales guys," I happily admit it — but I prefer to think that I get the maximum reward for the minimum effort and SBI! is an important part of that.)

When I think of all that SBI! does for me,

I'm amazed that you sell it for peanuts

First, it brings in super-targeted leads. Do you have any idea how much time and energy I would have to spend to do that without a Web site? I choke to think about it.

Second, it can help you look like a big organization with multiple warehouses across the country even though you work in your bathrobe in the den. And, in one sense, I really do have warehouses all over our nation. I just don't own them and don't have to worry about them.

Of course, it's also a brochure for all my products. I don't have to spend a penny printing or mailing brochures. And I don't have to waste a second, either. As soon as a lead finds my content, there's the brochure, product information, content, etc.

Fourth, it can also actually sell the products, too, and collect the money electronically. On my first site, we took payment via PayPal, smooth as silk, easy as pie.

Fifth, you build a bond with your customers. We had started an e-zine, a very professional-looking newsletter, with the first site. Our customers love the updates, and by staying in front of their eyeballs, they thought of Jerry Mack when they thought about their next purchase.

Naturally, we'll be doing all this again, too, with Sonomahealth.com. (By the time you read this, Sonomahealth.com may already have an online store where the products are sold using PayPal.)

So how's it going?

SonomaHealth recently broke inside the Top 200,000 Sites at Alexa.com. It's really just getting going, and I'll be building it up, pulling in lots more traffic.

And yes… I can tell you what that "Top 200,000" means already for my wife (who is not only my lifetime partner, but business partner, too) and me… we're already averaging $10,000 in commissions per month. Ken, we're running… and this time we own it!

One step at a time, I'll build Sonomahealth.com far bigger than my first effort. And you know what… I could do this in any number of industries. There is simply no reason for me, or any other reasonably ambitious person who wants to own their own life, to work a 9-to-5 anymore.

Thank you Ken! I have a great marketing positioning for you. You know the way Arnold S. called himself "The Terminator"? Well, you should be…

"The Liberator"
Jerry Mack
Sonoma Health Products, Inc.
sonomahealth.com

If Sales or Rentals are Your Passion, you can gain all the sales or leads that you need. Just provide high quality content about your products and targeted visitors will come to you seeking information. Once they have the information they need (the information that you provided) many will be ready to buy, as the next step on their journey. You will be there to provide them what they need!

Service Sellers

John Burch

Here is the story of John Burch, a local dental service provider, in his own words:

"A new patient (I'm removing her name due to patient confidentiality) just sent me this email to introduce herself and ask for an appointment. She is contacting me from Sacramento, which is 120 miles from my office!

> Subject: New Patient

> I live in Sacramento and found your website over the internet. It seems that your practice has a wonderful philosophy. I would love to come in for an appointment, I have pending dental work that needs to be done and I have severe dental phobia so I would love to come in for a visit. I am also interested in the Lumineers. Please let me know how I can schedule a visit.
>
> thanks again,
> Katie

Ken, that's powerful! It proves one of the great benefits of C-T-P-M. By reading thirty+ pages of my own content, the person can make sense of who I am and decide whether or not to trust me.

And we had a new patient yesterday ($19,500 cosmetic veneer case) who found us online and came all the way from Las Vegas!! (over 400 miles). Apparently, the power of C-T-P-M and SBI! has no limits!!!

Try THAT with a classified ad!!"

Best regards,

John Burch
drburch.com

If You Provide a Service, You are Selling Yourself. Trust is key in the services selling business, because who you are is intricately tied to the service that you provide. Your name, your credibility and your service are all in question. Give your visitors the information that they need to make a sound decision about you and what you provide, and your prospective clients will be beating a path to your door.

Students

What would it be like to start a business while you are in school; a business that you can operate from your laptop? A business that does not require you to talk to customers, accept credit cards, handle order processing, packaging or shipping products? What if the subject-matter of your business is the same as your major in school? What if you could run your business part-time, a few hours per week? What if all you needed to do was to write about what you love? What if the success of your business connected you to the people who are important in the industry you want to become a part of?

Nori Evoy

Here's more of Nori's story in her own words, she started when she was 14 years old:

"Who Would Have Thought That A Vacation Could Pay My Way Through University?

The beautiful. Caribbean island of Anguilla is a place not many people know about. My Dad hadn't.

And then he read a book. It is an inspiring story about two people selling everything they owned, "slowing down" and opening up their dream... a restaurant in Anguilla.

Their love of the island, through successes and mishaps, their description of the island and its people, caught my dad's fancy. This book is really about a journey down a "road less traveled."

It's really about people choosing to lead their own lives.

I feel so sad for people who are stuck working for people they don't like, for those who are forced to go to work, fight traffic, be in an office and then come home at the end of the day.

My dad works hard building SiteSell.com and SBI!. Probably too hard. But he loves what he does — I can see *his* dream, how SBI! can free people from a hum-drum life. You don't have to do what the Blanchard's did and risk every penny and open your own restaurant.

You can do what I did. But never meant to. ;-) (After all, who could have imagined that *A Trip to the Beach* and SBI! would turn me into a successful Web site owner, too?)

Anyway, all that to say... when my Dad asked me to write my "case study," how could I say "no"? (How could I say "no" anyway — but that's a different story!).

Before I start my story, I should add one thing... I get some e-mail saying how lucky I am to have my Dad tutor me on "Net marketing." Well, he doesn't.

He does help me a lot with my writing — he loves to write, and he pushes me to "say it better, Nori — make it come alive." And he did help me get started with the software. But I do all the rest myself.

My Story Begins

As I was saying, my Dad works pretty hard. But when we vacation, we *vacation.* No laptops. No cell phones. No RIM. Just tropical clothes and snorkeling equipment!

We had fallen in love with Anguilla on our first trip to the island. So a whole month in Anguilla was looking very appealing.

I won't bore you with the details of that trip, but if you know my Dad at all, you will have guessed that we pushed our car to corners of the island where even the locals never go. We ate, swam and drank (ahem, did I mention the rum punches?) it all.

About half way through that trip, I asked my Dad, "Would Anguilla be a good topic for a Web site?"

Uh-oh. The lights in my Dad's eyes went on.

"Nori, what a great idea."

He went on to explain how the World Wide Web is really nothing more than hundreds of millions of people looking for information, and millions of sites that provide that information. Except that most sites just try to make money with their sites... without providing what people look for... the information.

Anguilla would, he said, be a wonderful theme, for a site, if there was enough demand for information about Anguilla and not too much competition. If there was, then I could indeed attract visitors by providing good information (and we were becoming experts on Anguilla by now!). The final question, he said, was...

"Assuming you can build the traffic, how will you convert those visitors into revenue?"

In short, my Dad calls this...

Content > Traffic > PREsell > Monetize.

It all seemed pretty simple, when he explained it like that. We had a wonderful vacation. And my brain kept thinking about how this adventure would make a good Web page, or that restaurant, etc.

There was only one problem... I didn't know how to make a Web page!

Anguilla-Beaches.com Is Born

When we got home, my Dad showed me the Brainstormer software. Talk about amazing. Magic. And there were lots of great topics (called "keywords") about Anguilla. And not too much competition.

So we knew that we could build a site that would attract enough visitors who are interested in Anguilla. But as my Dad says, "There's no point in building a site, even one with traffic, if you don't have a plan for how you are going to convert that traffic into income, Nori. Unless you just want a hobby site, of course."

Now, I have nothing against those who just want to have a hobby site. But as long as you're going to write about something you know and love, you might as well earn some money to pay for Radiohead concerts and clothes, right?

As a student, I don't really have any services to sell. And I do not have time to create or sell products (although eventually I might write the *Xtreme Tourist Guide to Anguilla* book). And my Dad does not want me to e-mail with strangers, not for a couple more years, so no customer support he says.

However, he explained that there are a lot of local Anguillian businesses who do not have a Web site. Or if they do, they get no traffic and never will. So he explained how I could earn a finder's fee by sending clients to them.

In addition, I could be an affiliate and earn commissions by sending people to Amazon.com and Barnes & Noble to buy books on Anguilla. Google AdSense did not exist yet.

So, based on all our keyword brainstorming research and monetization plan, "Anguilla-Beaches.com" was born.

I read the Action Guide, which was long but easy-reading (in case you're wondering, my Dad is not saying whether that little Action Guide shadow-man with the hat and the whip is him or not). My Dad did help me through a couple of the sections, but that's more because he hovers — I could have done it all on my own.

His most important help was really to push me to write to "touch" my visitors. If you just write to make money, you will fail. If you write to truly touch and inform and please your visitors, good things will follow. That's a lesson that I will always have with me, and I don't just mean for anguilla-beaches.

I'll spare you the details of actually "doing SBI!," because it really was quite easy…

The Traffic Starts

I don't quite know how to say this next part. Have you ever worked on something, and you know it's supposed to work, but you don't somehow believe it?

Well, that's kind of like what I was doing.

First, let me back up a bit and tell you that I was afraid. I was scared that my Dad would think I was dumb because I had no idea how to write a Web page. I was afraid of failing… and somehow, I didn't really think "anyone would come."

"But if you don't try, you don't get." (Yes, you-know-who says that, too.)

Well anyway, I started writing Web pages, not wanting him to see them. My first two were up before he even knew it! It was so easy with the block-by-block builder. And the neat part is that the online help taught me some simple HTML, like how to make a word bold or navy blue.

My Dad was really impressed. We reviewed the pages and he showed me how to say things better. How to choose better words. How to close a page with more "punch." It all makes sense once it's explained to you, and now SBI! even includes sections on how to write like that!

Soon, I was using an HTML Editor called "BBEdit" (we use Macs). My Dad did help me a bit with this. But anyway, back to "believing." Guess what happened next?

People started visiting. First a few per day. Then tens, hundreds, more and more and more. And they loved the site. I received wonderful e-mail (my Dad has someone screen my e-mail — I think I'm old enough, but he worries about this, so I only see them and I don't reply to it).

I have received e-mail from…

— The Anguilla Tourist Board — "You go girl." That was great! They have written several times since, thanking me.

— Anguilla Life magazine — Claire Devener, the publisher, has become friends of the family.

— Many restaurants and spots around the island, thanking me for mentioning them.

— Hundreds of people who discovered Anguilla just because of the site.

— And I am even recognized on the beach... which is very weird.

Which brings me back to "believing." Although I understood what I was doing, somehow it is still amazing when you see yourself at #1 on Google for "anguilla beaches" and when you see visitors arriving, and especially when you see all the people you reach from all over the world.

My site even gets a higher traffic ranking than big, glitzy sites like arawakbeach.com, a local hotel site and anguilla-vacation.com, the Anguilla Tourist Board site.

When I stop to think about it, I still find it strange. But the reason is so simple... people return when you provide information that touches them. They subscribe to your e-zine. They find you at the engines because you offer so many pages that cover so many keywords. They find you... they like you... and they keep coming. Like my Dad said...

Content > Traffic > PREsell That has to come first.

It worked! And now...

Monetization

My Dad had explained to me how 98% of online business people focus on "getting the money" first. Only one problem. Their sites don't attract anyone!

Now that anguilla-beaches was getting traffic, my Dad arranged with another good friend and wonderful real estate agent, for me to earn a commission by referring real estate leads to her. I built an entire section on real estate — all those photos my Dad took came in handy!

As a results, she has sold a house and rented many villas (some of those villas rent for thousands of dollars per night). This single referer arrangement already earns most of my income from the site, and my Dad wants to arrange similar deals with other professionals and services and businesses on the island.

And I was accepted as a Google partner. The Google ads alone earn me a lot more than my friends who work part-time in fast food restaurants.

The affiliate income is the least important revenue generator, but it's better than nothing!

The End… Or The Beginning

We've made several trips to Anguilla since then… I know that's where my parents will settle when I'm in university. And every trip, we accumulate more and more great content.

I don't try to be all things to all people. There are other sites that are far more comprehensive. But people don't necessarily want "comprehensive." As my Dad says, "We live in an info-overloaded world, Nori. If you find the best for people and save them the time of having to read too much, you're providing real value."

So that's my niche… the best of Anguilla… from a family's point of view.

On this next trip, I'll use Form Build It! to add more lead-generating income for a boat charter, a tour operator, and other higher-end businesses. I'm not in a rush. It's important for me to find the right partner to recommend, not just to make money.

Oh, and speaking of money, I wasn't kidding about university. My Dad will, of course, help with university. But please don't think I'm one of those kids with a silver spoon in my mouth. My Dad refuses to spoil us and I guess that's why I called this section "The End… Or The Beginning."

This is the end of my story, but just the beginning of my adult life. I've learned that it takes some work to succeed. If you re-read my story, you'll see how important it is to work smart. That's more important than working hard.

SBI! did not build my site… it did not build my business. I did.

But it did help me to work smart. I picked a good theme, thanks to SBI!.

I built a Web site, which I could never have even started without it.

Traffic grew, thanks to SBI! leading me through the process of writing my words so that they make both my human visitors and the search engines happy. I had to work to do this, but I could not imagine doing it without SBI!.

SBI! took away 90% of the "work hard" and let me work smart.

I now have a business that I can grow over the years. A business that is fun. I'll never do a 9 to 5. I'll always own my own life.

That, more than money, more than learning about the Web, more than anguilla-beaches, more than learning how to write well, that is the most important thing I've learned from SBI!.

Own your own life. If you don't, what's the point?

Thank you, Dad

Nori Evoy
anguilla-beaches.com

Webmaster

Don Coggan

Here's the story of Don Coggan, a local webmaster, in his own words:

"In 1996, I left engineering management cold turkey to get into the exciting World Wide Web. I describe my business by saying that I'm an Internet

Business Consultant. This is to suggest that I do more than "webmastering." Around 2003 I heard about SBI!. Then, in early 2005, I REALLY discovered it. Since then I've converted most of my clients' and my own sites over to SBI!

My own sites were intended initially to test various hypotheses about what worked and what didn't work in terms of Internet marketing. I still use them for experimental purposes while at the same time making some money with them. The experimentation I've done has shown me that with SBI! I can enjoy the CERTAINTY of getting results. Without SBI!, I sort of knew what I was doing but I was never really sure about the outcome.

Without SBI!, I was more or less trying things to see if (hoping) they would work. Based on my experience with SBI!, I know the SBI! methods work, so now it's just a question of doing the work, without agonizing over whether something will work or not.

With my results-oriented philosophy, using SBI!, it's a LOT easier to sell my services to a potential client. It's also much easier to filter out the prospects that refuse to (or cannot) see a web site as anything more than an electronic brochure.

My advice to webmasters considering SBI! is to give it a fair try - as soon as possible. Contact other SBI! webmasters who are part of a community that so generously shares its experiences and offers advice. Above all, follow all the recommendations of the superb Action Guide. And if you're stubborn in your ways, as most of us webmasters seem to be, resist the urge to keep on doing things the way you've always done them!" ;-)

Don Coggan
Webmaster, Canada
coggan.com

Webmaster Double-Dip. All SBI! owners get a double-dip, but since a webmaster functions as a consultant to people who are seeking information about websites and how to create them successfully, SBI! makes perfect sense and cents! Your website brings lots and lots of traffic from people who want to know more about websites, your website provides them with high quality content, and the SBI! affiliate program helps you to earn income from those that choose to join you as SBI! owners.

Work at Home Moms

Here is a work at home mom and her story about building three businesses with SBI!

Tracy Achen

How did you come up with your site theme(s)?

"After reading the action guide (which tells you to focus on something that you are passionate about) I chose to focus on the subject of divorce from a woman's perspective. After being emotionally and financially devastated by my divorce, this was something that I was definitely passionate about. I wanted to help other women prepare for and understand the divorce process so that they could avoid some of the mistakes that I had made.

I started my credit site later that year after seeing the income potential from commission off of credit cards. After doing extensive research on the keywords, I decided to have the site encompass the major areas surrounding credit. This is because each area affects the other. Basically, I offer general credit advice, information about credit reports, and a system to find different credit cards. This is a constantly evolving website.

My last website I built due to the conviction that the SBI! system is the best way to create a website. It offers the basics of how to build your own website and what you should consider along the way. This site is really fun to work on because it makes me go back and review what I have done on the other two websites, helping me to make changes to improve them. They say that the best way to really learn a subject is to teach it, and this has certainly been true in my case."

What was your motivation for starting an online business?

"After my divorce, I was financially strapped and looking for some extra income. I had gotten interested in a MLM venture, but was disappointed that I would have to pay outrageous fees for a website that I had no control over. This began my journey for information about starting my own website which I could have total control over."

How long was it before you found success with your site(s)? Please define what "success" means to you.

"My first year, I was able to see a small profit with my divorce website, but my real success came in the form of positive feedback from my visitors. Women across the country and the world were letting me know that my website was making a difference in their lives. I admit that it takes a lot of time answering their emails, but this was something that I chose to do from the beginning.

In fact, had I known how much time this aspect would take, I probably wouldn't have ever started in the first place. Luckily, I didn't know. The fact that I can truly help other women far outweighs the efforts involved. The letters from the women make it all worth it.

I need to point out that not all websites require so much email support. The divorce site does because there is such a wide variation in divorce law from state to state. The questions to my credit site are really basic in nature. In fact, I will probably be adding a FAQS section that answers all these questions. And I really don't get that many questions from other site because I try to provide the information that they are seeking directly on the website.

I measure success with my credit site by the commissions that I make, but I also know that I am providing relevant information due to the steady increase in traffic that I get. My success on www.makeyourownwebsiteguide.com comes through the sharing of information. I'm steadily building traffic and subscribers, which in turn will lead to revenue as I begin to monetize it at some point in time.

What is your average monthly income?

"$1857/mo. For January 2005, my income was $1409. In September 2005, my income was $2943. Generally, there has been a steady climb in income each month."

What monetization models do you use?

"78% of the money I make is through affiliate commissions. Basically, I post links to merchant sites, and they pay me a commission when someone purchases from them. Also included in this figure is income from Google Adsese, but it's not a great amount due to the fact that it's only on a few of my pages. 14% of my income is from the sale of my book about divorce, and I also make 8% from directory listing fees from the lawyers who list their services on my site."

How many hours per week do you work on your site(s)?

"I spend approximately 40 hours a week on my website (I know, same as a regular job), but I am able to be home for the kids. I can help them with their homework and listen as they talk about their day."

What is your pre-SBI! work experience? Include both WAH and outside experience.

"As I look back over my work history, I've spent about 15 years of my life cleaning something. I've cleaned out animal stalls, new-construction homes, occupied houses, and washed cars (about 1500 per week). During my separation and divorce, I decided that it was about time to do something that wasn't dependent on the weather and paid a regular paycheck, so I started working as a magazine merchandiser. I like the flexibility of my work, but the pay left a lot to be desired. I was making about $700 a month and trying to support my family.

Struggling to pay the bills is what got me to thinking about earning some extra income, which eventually lead me to where I am now. I started my website while I was still working. This way, if it flopped, I still had my job. I continue to build it along the way, eventually adding two more websites. I had a work injury in 2003 and had to eventually quit my job in 2004. Even though it was scary letting go of the security of a paycheck, it was the best decision that I ever made. I've been able to devote my time and attention to my websites, and the effort is paying off."

What "sold" you on SBI!? What would you change?

"I got my first "real" computer (the first was a DOS) in 1999, so I really didn't have a lot of experience using a computer. What sold me on SBI! was the fact that I didn't need to be a computer geek to build my website. All I had to do was pick my template to get the basic look for my website, and be able to copy and paste my information into the building blocks. What I like so much about SBI! is that it includes everything that I need, without having to use a lot of outside programs.

For example, I don't have to go to every search engine to submit my pages and check my rankings. When I add a new page to my website, SBI! analyzes it to make sure that I have it optimized for the search engines (this way I don't have to keep tweaking my page to get higher rankings). I am able to get the relevant data that I need for traffic analysis and reciprocal linking.

Another added bonus is the email system that filters out all the spam, saving me countless hours of hitting the delete button. There are so many things that SBI! does for me that I would never consider switching.

At times I thought it would be nice to have SSI (server side includes) capabilities so that I could make universal changes across the website without having to edit every page. But the way it is now also has its' benefits. When I want to make such a change on all my pages, I am able to re-analyze and update my pages on an individual basis so that they perform better. If I were to be able to push one button to change everything, those pages might just gather dust and become outdated."

If you could go back, what would you do differently with your website(s)?

"If I could go back, I really wouldn't change a thing. Granted, what I started with was not exactly flashy, but I was able to communicate my messages in a way that real people could relate to. It's funny, I started my credit site because I saw how much money could be made on credit cards, but as the site evolved, I found myself again in the position of helping people, only this time it was helping people understand the basics of credit.

When you focus your website on helping others, you truly are a winner. The money is just secondary."

How do you "do it all" (i.e. childcare, housework, meals, play, etc.)?

"When I first started out, I had to save working on my website until after the kids went to bed or on weekends. The thing is, it never really seemed like work to me. It was fun and challenging at the same time, with me often finding it hard to tear myself away from the computer. As the kids got older, I was able to spend more time on it during the early evening. Once I quit my job, I was able to work on it during the school hours. I take small breaks from the computer to do laundry, clean, walk the dogs, etc.

I could probably cut down on the number of hours that I spend developing my websites, but I don't want to. It excites me and gives me a broader purpose. I am more than just a wife and mother. My oldest son has even bragged that his mom owns and develops websites (this is really big considering that he is a teenager). I'm lucky that my kids and new husband support me, and that I have found something that is so fulfilling."

Tracy Achen
New Mexico, United States
womansdivorce.com (started January 2001)
creditsourceonline.com (started September 2001)
makeyourownwebsiteguide.com (March 2003)

Here is another work at home mom and her story about creating a business with SBI!

Nicole Tod

What is your pre-SBI! work experience? Include both WAH and outside experience.

"I am British and started my career as a nurse which was something I had wanted to do since I was about 5 years old. I can still vividly remember regularly setting up my toy ironing board with all my plastic tools and giving my parents 'foot care'! Consequently I went on to train as a nurse which led to school nursing then pediatric nursing and finally I became a Health Visitor.

After 10 years of nursing I was ready for a different challenge and so off I went to work in a refugee camp in Sudan. That was one of the most challenging and rewarding things that I have ever done and the kindness and gratitude of all the people that I worked with will stay with me forever. Another great thing to come out of my stay in Sudan was that I met my husband Bill. He too was working with the same organization (Save the Children). One thing led to another and hey presto, here we are happily married and with three great kids.

Moving on several years…

Bill is still working with Save the Children and we have been working and living overseas now for thirteen years - Togo, Ghana, Mali, Vietnam and latest stop is Bangkok. We love it all and although I have not been working regularly per se (not always easy to get work when you are on the move every three years) I have felt immensely privileged to be able to stay at home and bring up my kids."

What education and/or training do you have?

"I finished full time school education at 18 years of age. This was followed by 3 years basic nurse training, 1 year pediatric nurse training, 18 months health visitor training then just for something different I did 2 correspondence courses in interior design and setting up a home based business and then a 2 year diploma in French."

Do you currently work outside the home?

"No, unless you can count unpaid work such as supermarket shopping and acting as a taxi service for my kids!"

What was your motivation for starting an online business versus other WAHM options?

"As we move location every 3 years or so, it was important that any business that I did was mobile. I love working my way round the internet and have dabbled with several web design programs – very unsuccessfully until I discovered SBI!. I also love children and being creative with them so I felt that my website was the perfect answer to put all my skills and interests together."

How long have you been with SBI!?

"2 years."

How did you discover SBI!?

"By chance in my quest to set up a home based business. I think it was on one of those WAHM websites."

What "sold" you on SBI!?

"Initially it got my interest as the SBI! site was different from the others in that I felt I was being talked to rather than talked at. It wasn't so high-tech and frightening as many of the other sites and somehow seemed to be answering most of my question that I had in my head. I downloaded the free eBook and read it thoroughly but was still confused a little and I suppose nervous about spending on something that I really had no idea about – I had never heard of affiliate marketing until then.

I suppose what really cemented my decision to go with SBI! was when I emailed Judd a load of question and worries and he came straight back with some great advice and answers. I realized then that SBI! was not some mechanical site and system and that there were real people behind it who were ready to help me get started and to support me as I went along."

How did you convince your "significant other" that SBI! (or an online business) was a viable option for your family?

"Easily. My husband was happy to see me doing something that I enjoy and is already planning his early retirement!"

How does your "significant other" support you? Do you have advice to offer other WAHM's on eliciting support from "significant others"?

"My husband is great on excel and writing emails but that is about it. So, technically he doesn't support me at all but where he is good at is just listening to me prattle on about my day and what I have achieved (or not!). I think my advice to others would be not to bore the pants off your family like I have done in the past. My website topic doesn't particularly 'excite' my husband so I tend to get friends or other family members to critique pages. Be prepared though for both positive and negative comments. Sometimes I have spent hours putting up a great page only for someone to suggest I could have done it differently."

Are your kids involved with SBI! and your business? If so, how?

"My kids are involved directly and indirectly. Indirectly as a lot of the advice I give my visitors is drawn from experience of the parties that I have thrown for my kids. Whereas directly they are involved in testing out some of the craft projects that I suggest (photos of their projects usually make it on to my web pages) and in suggestion ideas for different party themes that they would like."

How did you come up with your site theme(s)?

"It took me a while as initially I couldn't see what I was good at or what interested me the most. However once I started following the action guide, I was able to see that a website doesn't have to be about something hi-tech or be just a sales site and that the idea of kids parties was literally staring me in the face."

How long was it before you found success with your site(s)? Please define what "success" means to you.

"That's a tricky one to answer. I suppose for me there were/are several levels of success and each one is related to the goals that I set myself. The first element of success for me was just the fact of setting up a web site. After all my failed attempts in the past, the achievement that I felt when I got my first page up is indescribable. The second element of success for me was when I started to earn some money. I can vividly remember my first earnings – all of 4 cents! But oh boy was I happy. Last month I had earned enough to buy a laptop computer – that felt like success!

Now that I have achieved the above 2, my success goals have changed. Firstly I plan to develop my party themes and my party entertainer's directory, then I want to write an eBook and finally I am setting myself monetary goals for the year ahead. I think with a web business, your goals and what you consider successful can change all the time and as you achieve one thing, you set yourself another target. So in a nutshell for me, success is achieving the goals that I set for myself no matter how big or small."

What is your average monthly income?

"For the past 6 months my average earnings have been around $335 USD per month."

Which monetization models do you use?

"It took me a while to monetize and initially I was jumping the gun and doing things too early which only set me back in the long run. Now I feel more settled and confident and am concentrating on a few monetization strategies.

Basically I use Google Adsense (Just love it); am listed in a few directories; affiliate marketing; link exchange (been difficult to find decent links which aren't direct competition); started an e-zine about 4 months ago (I find that a bit of a struggle); I have written 2 articles for e-zine directories (got me lots of traffic) and my latest is setting up a party entertainers directory. At present I provide free listings but I may charge a small fee in the future as it is very, very time consuming."

How many hours per week do you work on your site(s)?

"I spend far too many and some days I feel and look very cross-eyed. I would say about 4 hours a day Monday to Friday. Never in the evenings and never at the weekends as that is family time."

How do you "do it all" (i.e. childcare, housework, meals, play, etc.)? Please provide tips for other SBI! WAHM's—ideas that have worked for you.

"I am embarrassed to say that I have someone who does most of the housework for me. It is not as luxurious as it sounds as we live in Asia and it is the norm to have some home help who will do the ironing, cleaning and washing. If I didn't have that help, I honestly don't know how I would manage. Setting up and maintaining a successful website is not something that you just dabble in when you have a few minutes to spare. It does take time and commitment."

If you could go back, what would you do differently with your website(s)?

"I would narrow down my main topic. I feel my topic on kid's parties is too wide to do successfully and thoroughly. I would maybe have just stuck to party themes or party games."

Please feel free to add any other pearls of wisdom you feel would be helpful to other moms!

"My advice would be to research thoroughly before you spend a dime. Check out other web hosting and building programs before you get SBI!. That way you will realize what an excellent deal SBI! really is. Also you may find something more suited to your needs.

Don't get into affiliate marketing for the money. Few people make much money in the first couple of years. After two years I make what I call "Holiday money". In other words it will pay for our family holidays. I am very happy with that I might add.

Be realistic. It takes up more of your time than you think, especially in the first year.

Create your own private workspace which is especially for you. Tidy it up each day as it is amazing how quickly it becomes a mess and then your mind is all over the place.

If you are short on time, prioritize. Write a list of what is important and stick to it. It is so easy to get carried away with browsing the forums or playing around with images when you might be better off getting a decent paragraph up on one of your pages.

Make use of the forums. I cannot tell you how much they have helped me. Now I try to put something back into them although lately I have been a bit absent as we are packing up for yet another house move – we are going to live in Hanoi for 3 years and we arrive a couple of days before Christmas.

It is very easy to become totally unsociable and boring when you are spending a long time on the computer. Try to set times when you will not work such as weekends or when the kids arrive home from school.

I could write more but the kids are about to pounce through the door, I have to get to the supermarket, the turtle is going to the vets, I have packing boxes strewn around the house, I need a cup of tea......and I haven't had my daily dose of lurking round the SBI! forum (5 minutes only I promise).

Nicole Tod
Thailand but soon moving to Hanoi, Vietnam
kids-partycabin.com

Teaching SBI!

Are you a teacher, a professor, or a person with a passion to become one? Once you've created a site (even a site dedicated to teaching SBI!) you could offer the SiteSell Education course in colleges, universities or continuing education programs. The Site Build It! course is offered in numerous colleges and universities nationwide, including The University of Arizona, Penn State and the Citadel.

If you become an instructor, you can earn a teaching fee from each student, as well as, bulk SBI! subscription commissions, additional site sales, bulk renewals, more income since the buzz you create from your excited SBI! students will generate new business for you locally, and even more revenue because you become the local "go-to" person, thanks to your high-profile association with a group.

The combination of SBI! commissions and teaching fees is a excellent combination. Every class you teach could easily generate $2000-$3000, based on commissions and class fees, all for 40-50 hours of work. That's $60 per hour. And that's all money in YOUR pocket. If you were to conduct two classes a month, you could earn $4,000 to $6,000, in addition to the renewals that would occur each year.

SiteSell Services

SiteSell Services can build, or build and manage your website for you if you do not have the time, or do not want to do it yourself. In addition to building a site for you, a specialist can work with you to add keyword-focused content pages to your site on a regular basis, or to do any custom work that you would like performed on your site.

SiteSell Affiliate Program

Finally, as a SBI! site owner, you can earn commissions from visitors who sign-up with SBI! as a result of a relationship that you have created. I am a SBI! affiliate, as well as a site owner. If you are interested in becoming a SBI! owner, please visit my SBI! page to see more details, great videos, ask me questions or sign-up. I welcome you to become part of the community that has changed many lives, and could change your life, too!

Want More SBI!

Please visit my site here: http://www.free-job-search-websites.com/sbi-site-build-it.html. You can find out more SBI! info, ask me questions directly, watch the SBI! videos, or simply get started!

If you are as excited about SBI! as I was, contact me for a special offer before you sign-up with SBI!

http://free-job-search-websites.com/sbi-site-build-it-special-offer.html

Book Notification

If you would like to receive news about new book launches and free book offers, sign up here:

http://www.free-job-search-websites.com/amazon.html

Other Books by Lee Evans

— *Killer Work from Home Jobs: 200 Fortune 500 & Legitimate Work at Home Jobs*

— *Killer Work from Home Jobs 2: 100 Fortune 500 & Legitimate Work at Home Jobs*

— *Killer Work from Home Jobs: 460 Jobs SUPER* BOOK

Future Books by Lee Evans

— *Killer Work from Home Jobs for Bloggers*

— *Killer Work from Home Jobs for Writers*

— *Killer Work from Home Jobs for Information Technology*

— *Killer Work from Home Jobs International*

Made in the USA
Monee, IL
04 November 2026

67387911R00056